Stroking the Zebra?

Part 1 "How and why do I think as I do"
Part 2 "What do I think about from A to Z"

ROBERT LESLIE CORRON
iUniverse, Inc.
New York   Bloomington

iUniverse books may be ordered through booksellers or by contacting:

iUniverse
1663 Liberty Drive
Bloomington, IN 47403
www.iuniverse.com
1-800-Authors (1-800-288-4677)

Because of the dynamic nature of the Internet, any Web addresses or links contained in this book may have changed since publication and may no longer be valid. The views expressed in this work are solely those of the author and do not necessarily reflect the views of the publisher, and the publisher hereby disclaims any responsibility for them.

ISBN: 978-1-4401-8578-6 (sc)
ISBN: 978-1-4401-8579-3 (ebook)

Printed in the United States of America

iUniverse rev. date: 3/2/2010

Contents

Dedication Page

My first dedication is to my parents, thanking them for my genetic heritage, and if it is true that the moral/ethical, right/wrong rules are set before one is five years old, I thank them for those guide lines, because I seem to operate within excepted range in these areas, even given some environmental, experience or cultural pushes in contra directions.

My Next dedication is to Buck Lane; who, when everyone else thought I was broken, taught me to play chess and introduced me to the concepts of truth, kindness and justice. He died at Anzio. That was the last time I cried for myself. All my tears since then come from/for other people's stories.

I also dedicate the discourse to my three wives, the first who showed me that I just couldn't make it happen by my will, and second who taught be not to be in love with love, and the third, Bessie, who gave me the honor and pleasure of realizing what love and marriage could and should be. Without her, neither I nor this discourse would be here.

My last dedication is to all the other people who influenced my life in any way good or bad, but mostly those involved with my final work place environment, Computer Language Research, a small company in Carrollton (Dallas) Texas:

First to Roger, who hired me and listened to my Ramblings.

Next to Rick, who was just my friend, and showed me about personal strength in unique social situations.

And to Bonita, who had inner beauty, strength and Grace.

And to Joe, who taught me to curb my hyperbole and exaggerational rhetoric, that I didn't need it to be accepted, my work spoke for it self.

And to Glenn, who was my boss, who taught me to role play e.g., When a person in a committee meeting just didn't get it, I was not supposed to say "Hey, dumb ass, didn't you read the reports"; but to say instead, "Maybe the data was not formatted in the most understandable manner; lets approach this from another angle". In a word, he took a lump of rough coal and polished off the rough edges and put me under enough pressure to turn me into the diamond that was an aid to him and his programs, and not a hindrance.

And last, but by no means least, Charlie, who not only listened, but had the audacity to correct and mentor me when I strayed to far from reality.

Preface

This document is a methodology for trying to understand how I think and why I think as I do.

My thinking process is premise based.

I operate on the premise that evolutional genetic traits have more or less programmed the basic capabilities and limitations of the starting (initial) conditions of my particular "Human Nature".

From this point – Considering the environmental conditions from conception through embryology – all internal -> external responses are learned – given full consideration to the capabilities and limitations mentioned above, of my personal "Human Nature".

I also operate; in the philosophical mode – which I try to maintain at all times, on the premise that I am finite.

Being finite limits the data available for making absolute, truthful observations, and therefore decisions.

This being the case, I cannot believe or disbelieve anything.

Knowing that one cannot function in this limbo, I have formulated premises that I live by. They are somewhat found depending on new data or current situations.

Because of this I find that my premises are sometimes conflicting and contrary to one another. That is just the way it is, I live with it.

Acknowledgments

In my lifetime, I have read, read at, or read about, at least several thousand books, along with movies & TV, these are the data base(s) that are a large part of who I am.

I have read westerns, mysteries, historical novels, science fiction and fantasy, history, do it your self, self improvement, philosophy, poetry, mathematics, and lately, mainly, popularized science.

I now have a small library of about five hundred books covering most genres: that I have read or read at. This is not to brag, but just to let the reader know where my external operating data base came from.

I currently have more than on hundred books that popularize science, that I have listed in detail in Appendix 1.

Prologue

While researching book layouts, I discovered that the preface was the jumping off place for most books, but the "Prologue" was the start of a discourse.

The present document is a discourse stated in conversational first person format and there is a lot of "I" and "me" involved.

This discourse is based on the analysis of fifty seven arbitrary dichotomies that I hope will cover all facets of why and how I think the way I do.

I intended the dichotomies to be standalone pieces, but on review (and while writing them) I found that they overlap, are sometimes redundant, some time attacking a point from a different perspective and even conflicting and contradictory based on situational content.

I don't find this odd, because while I didn't realize it before I started this discourse, that's exactly how I think.

Another emerging property, if you will, also came out of this writing. Not only how and why I think as I do, but also what I think about certain areas of the human condition.

I therefore, plan to add some thoughts about some of those areas at the end of the discourse.

Starting Notes

This process will use the Dichotomy, Trichotomy, Polychotomy, and a Morphochotomy, as in The Dialectic, as a basis for analyzing how and why I think as I do.

The present states of my knowledge base are the unknowable, the knowable but unknown, and the known.

For my purpose; in this discourse, I will name (arbitrarily - by definition) and describe these systems in a reductional methodology.

The system of the first principle is the universe (cosmos). For descriptive purpose only, I will name the chain of systems according to their makeup.

The initial (starting?) conditions of the universe are (at this time) unknowable and I call them systems of dynamic chaos, without definable parameters or basic parts, and their capabilities and limitations (see the second dichotomy).

This is the Alpha System: Chaos without parameters, but deterministic, without predestination.

As this is not a study of the origin and metamorphous of the universe, I will jump to the present and describe the systems that make up the basics for my knowledge bases.

Chaotic, complicated, complex and simple:

Chaotic: A set of results seemingly arrived at through random processes with some stable facets that indicate that the process is not totally random, but at this time unknown and darkly opaque.

Complicated: An opaque system made up of complex subsystems that the connections and feedback processes are partially unknown but knowable.

Complex: A translucent system, made up of simple systems whose feed back processes are knowable and controllable.

Simple: A transparent system of known input, processes. Feedback and output.

The above is broad overview of the areas that this discourse will investigate i.e., in order to go from the simple to the chaotic or the chaotic to the simple one must employ the dichotomies and their complex makeup.

A basic premise of all that follows is that man (I): the story teller; in discrete steps of either/or, manipulates his environment, both physical and mental, individually or collectively.

Digital and Analog

Digital and Analog is probably the primary dichotomy.

Digital has to do with discrete and static parts that make up a whole or complete subject and/or system and can be considered grainy and/or lumpy, while Analog is at the same time continuous and complete.

This is a broad dichotomy, and is reflected in almost all the dichotomies that follow.

Digital and Analog are liken to Quantum Mechanics and Classical Physics, in that the former operates with quanta and the latter operates as if gear driven.

The Digital calculator and/or computer operate with bits in the on or off mode, while the Analog calculator and/or computers are driven by gears and levers.

Digital and Analog can also be associated with Time and Space, where Time is made up of a collection of discrete moments and Space is a continuous whole or on the other hand time can be assumed continuous and space can be described as a special set of discrete coordinates?

It has been said that the left brain is Digital and the right brain is Analog.

It all depends on the point of view and the desired result one wishes to present at any given time or place.

It is like most dichotomies and coins; they have two sides that reflect the eyes of the beholder.

All the above is a preamble to all that follows; mostly, what you see is what you get, right or wrong?

Capabilities and Limitations

For this discourse, and for all practical purposes, everything is a system with some inputs, processes, feedback and output.

The Capabilities and Limitations of these simple systems are a function of their design or makeup.

They are able to take up/in some specific input/data from an external source and process this data/info into a programmed/defined output.

In a simple system there is no emerging properties, that is, there is no gestalt result, i.e., it is equal to the sum of it parts.

Therefore the Capabilities of a system are the value of the input less the cost of processing.

Also the Limitations of the system are related to the value and completeness of the input, the efficiency of the process and feedback loops and the natural parameters of physical possibility.

When describing the Capabilities and Limitations of something, those above statements are not always apparent, because most something's are not simple systems, but at best complex or complicated or at worse chaotic or seemingly random.

In broad, general terms, the Limitations of a system are the functions of the natural laws.

On the other hand, because the parameters of the natural laws are so vast, the Capabilities of systems are, also vast, almost beyond comprehension.

For the purpose of this dichotomy; and perhaps all the rest, I am trying to come to a dialectic balance between Capabilities and Limitations.

The Dialectic: from thesis vs antithesis to synthesis, i.e., the desired Capabilities or Limitations of reality and the working compromise between the two.

As the aim of this entire discourse is to investigate how I think and why I think as I do, and how can I improve on my current methodologies, the above is all about my inputs; filtered through my personal version of human nature, i.e., my genetic makeup, and from all the acquired data of the past that I have been exposed to, and my interpretation of it, processed through my cognitive centers and into my awareness and consciousness, and what are the Capabilities and Limitations of this process.

Cause (laws) and Effect (results)

I am finite; I have a beginning, duration and an end.

There is a cause or law(s) behind the starting conditions of this beginning, and these laws (the cause) are both the input and processing of my finite system; in this case a complex/complicated system, and the output is the effect.

Now, carry this over to a broad area of events.

Given that each event can be described as discrete and static, a priori to its duration, the cause(s) of this event is (are) the results of effects of prior or contemporary discrete events.

The point is; although, I and other events may be finite, I (they) are part of an infinite regression, and therefore the starting conditions of these events are the output or effects of a set of the initial conditions of the onset of the space/time continuum.

Another point here, in relation to the purpose of this discourse on how and why I think as I do, is not to get caught up in the idea that, although each event is discrete, and at a point static, that they (it) are/is not connected to some other more complex system or subsystem.

In other words, in (when) establishing a mental or physical/real plan, I do not get caught up in the idea that I have all the data available to predict the outcome of the plan.

The above is the basis for operating from a premise i.e., I am finite, the universe is for all practical purposes, related to me, infinite, therefore I do not have enough data available to my cognitive event horizon to know the whole truth; therefore, I cannot believe or disbelieve anything, either internal or external to myself. It is obvious that I cannot function in this mode; therefore, it is necessary for me to set up premises from which to operate i.e., I will assume in this or that given context, that this or that is so, and in the vernacular "believe" this the truth and operate on/from it.

I know that this is operating in a shadow world, but I have found that it is the only way to remain fluid/liquid in my thought processes.

This theme, like many others will be redundant throughout this discourse, because I "believe" that there are a limited number of laws (causes) that lead to the effects of our actions.

Deterministic and Predestined

By definition, deterministic systems operate relatively free within a set of parameters defined by the natural laws of physics and time.

At an extreme, one must say that these parameters are Predetermined by the initial (Starting?) conditions of the universe, while understanding, that for all practical purposes, relative to my finite self, is infinite.

This understood - the possibilities of actions are virtually unlimited, within these parameters.

On the other hand, Predestination is not varied or able to operate over a range.

Under the "Classical Physics" definition of Predestination, if one were able to define the states of all the particles in space/time, by their location and velocity at anytime, one could predict the past and future without error.

In a Deterministic system, there are degrees of freedom of choice and free will, while in a Predetermined system there is not, what will be, will be.

Heredity and Environment

Heredity is, by definition, genetically driven.

This is a simple statement that overlays a very complex situation.

Each organism has a genome of various size and Capabilities and Limitations.

For the most part; however, when Heredity and Environment are discussed, the subject under discussion is the human organism and in the case of the discourse, me.

Each new human organism, being the result of sexual activity, is the result of the combining of chromosomes of the two parents; therefore, reflecting a certain measure of both parents.

Due to the various and sundry potential errors, caused by copying, mutation or damage; environmental damage, that will be more defined and redefined in the discourse on Nature and Nurture, and the mutually exclusive and/or potentially variable traits of the re-combination of chromosomes; the process named meiosis, the new creation is not only a merged clone of the parents, but a unique variation of the genetic line.

For the purposes of this portion of the discourse, this definition covers the new organism from conception to birth.

The post natal phase of the new organism is now more or less controlled by the environment in which it is raised, keeping in mind the Capabilities and Limitations of the activity range defined by heredity.

Environment, by definition, includes food, clothing, shelter, care, love and all the other aspects of nurturing.

It also includes education, culture and the various aspects of world environment; pollution, climate, hazardous materials and political and social situations.

All the above is also tempered by the Capabilities and Limitations of the individual organism to adapt to and take advantage of the opportunities presented, whether they are beneficial to the organism or not.

This is a very broad definition that will be more defined and redefined; as stated above, in the discourse on Nature and Nurture.

Nature and Nurture

By definition, for the purposes of this dichotomy, Nature and Nurture will be defined and delineated in the pre-birth cycle of the organism.

Nature will cover the genetic factors involved with the organism, and Nurture will cover the functions and input from the host mother.

The nature function: in sexual reproduction starts with meiosis, the combination and merging of the parental somatic cells; half from each parent, to form the gamete within the female egg.

This is the step in the process that allows/generates the changes for variation in the new organism from either or both parents.

Another facet of the variation process is mutation, the altering of the genetic sequence in some manner in each or either of the germ (somatic) cells from the parents.

The last facet is copying errors, possibly caused by a lack of needed resources in the female egg?

If any of these steps fall out of very narrow parameters, the new organism is either born with defects or aborted.

For my purposes, the production of the viable (not aborted) gamete is the final step in the Nurture stage of the reproduction cycle.

The Nurture process is totally driven by the host mother and her internal and external environment.

In order for the genetic data/information/criteria to be fulfilled at the maximum level, leaving the new organism with the maximum (genetic driven) Capabilities and Limitations, the host mother must supply the demanded nutrients and environmental resources that the genetic code prescribes in order to produce the correct proteins and supporting systems e.g., enzymes, catalysts, mitochondria, etc. etc.

Variations can take place during this phase (usually detrimental mutations), caused by toxic materials e.g., drugs, pollutants, radiation and bad diet.

All of the above considered, if the new organism is birthed, the probability of survival to carry on and reproduce fall into the function of the Heredity/Environment cycle.

See the discourse on Heredity and Environment.

Positive and Negative

This sounds like the easiest of all dichotomies, but covers a wide range of meanings and situations.

Although some of the past and future discourses on dichotomies will/be/have been between philosophical, political, academic or scientific themes, this one will be mostly in dictionary mode, but nonetheless important, in the sense of "How and Why I Think as I Do".

The connotation that one puts on data or data points, depends on the various aspects of each, in a given dichotomy, under a given or even a fluid/liquid situation.

Positive or negative applies to the basic yes and no aspects of physical and/or mental situations.

It also applies to the results of various types of testing e.g., a test for cancer or some other kind of disease; a negative test is a good thing while on the other hand, for hopeful parents, a pregnancy positive is a good thing.

On the mathematical number line positive or negative are defined by distance or increments a number is from zero (0).

In particle physics and chemistry, positive and negative are associated with the attractive or repulsive attributes of the charges of various particles, molecules or compounds, and the ramifications of these charges in the relationship with the makeup of complex matter and/or energies. In other words, the very make up of our existence.

While in personal or personality matters they have to do with the ups and downs in ones psychic profile, so the dichotomy of positive and negative is transposed into the dichotomy of up and down, which also relates to back and forth, a relationship aligned with both direction and frequency.

The point of all the above is to emphasize the vast array and matrix Capabilities (and Limitations) of my language/cognitive/mental/verbal interpretation systems, that allows me to maintain a specific train of thought utilizing the positive and negative (excite and inhibit) impulses between the synapses in my neural systems.

So, I lied (or misstated the facts), this dichotomy is also philosophical and/or academic. I guess they all will be; no matter how hard I try to keep it simple, the emerging properties will (or may be) complex, complicated and/or chaotic, with special attractors that we can use to follow the discourse (dichotomy)??

Simple and Complex

For my purposes, in this discourse, I will start with Simple and Complex Systems.

A Simple System has one input flow, one process and one output, in its most basic form, and is transparent.

A system can still be Simple if its processing portion has a feedback loop (an, if then do, loop) that sets and either/or function that still ends up with one output.

A complex System is comprised of two or more Simple Systems, where the output of the first is the input of the second and so on, and my have alternate outputs. A Complex System may be transparent or translucent.

A basic, Simple System is the turnstile; it allows one person to pass through at a time.

A basic Complex turnstile System can have a counting process e.g., it can punch a hole in a tape as each person passes through.

A turnstile can still be just a Complex System, if you have to put in a coin to activate it, to allow one person to pass through, while still punching the tape to keep count.

From another point of view, simple things are straight forward and linier, such as require just a yes or no answer.

If, in a given situation, the answer is maybe, or if (the, if do loop) they still may be simple or they may be complex depending on the inclusion of another Simple System.

The point of this dichotomy is to asses the range of causes and responses, implied and/or directed from a given situation.

The cause and effect of a simple situation is straight forward, with little or no question of what follows, while on the other hand a complex situation, although still operating within controllable bounds, often requires more than one (or a choice of more than one) response or action.

In addition, in the areas of Trichotomy and Polychotomy, there are complicated systems/situations that are made up of multiples of simple and/or complex events/systems/situations that are opaque and often hard to follow, and then the chaotic systems/situations that are so dense that the activities or results are termed random.

The very basis of the Simple/Complex dichotomy discourse is to delineate, explain, define or otherwise examine the basic data/information flows that make up my thinking, and the outcome of inputs or sets of inputs, and what happens internally if the processes are overloaded with complex, complicated or chaotic inputs.

What is the cause of irrational thinking and activity?

Is it; a simple breakdown of the processes, or an inability to process conflicting data/information, and most importantly, can I somehow control the conflict by understanding the Simple/Complex functions, inputs and/or processes?

Very circular, chaotic, but really not random situations have much to do with the reason for this discourse (dichotomy) in the first place.

The Dialectic – Thesis, Antithesis & Synthesis

The Dialectic is one of the greatest philosophical analylictic concepts in modern history and part of my view of Trichotomy, Polychotomy and Morphochotomy.

An insight into how evolution, through natural selection and adaptation retained those organisms that were able to quickly analyze the current data/information from two perspectives; fight or flight, and choose the one that complemented survival and reproductive success.

In the initial modern usage in philosophy the dialectic allow(ed)(s)the linier presentation of two (or more [Trichotomy and Polychotomy]) contesting ideas and/or points of view, in order to come to a compromise (Morphochotomy) position by taking the best and most salient from both the thesis and antithesis and to reach synthesis.

Although, seemingly transparent, it is the backbone and underlying process of decision making in politics, business and everyday life.

It was always in my makeup, in the back round, but until the conceptualization and vocalization of the process, thesis, antitheses, and synthesis – the dialectic, was an unconscious and uncontrollable operation; helpful, but not maximized.

This conceptualization may be or have been the first step toward my ability to harness, at the conscious level, the very attributes of the unconscious processing that allowed me to evolve to my present state.

An insight, if you will, into the very fabric of consciousness.

Followed further into the innermost reaches, one may be able to grasp and operate on the first principle of existence and therefore be able to maximize the potential of the creative forces.

Biological Evolution
and Cultural Evolution

Biological Evolution and its propensity toward variation, seems to be the main force behind sustained life on earth (and anywhere else it emerges and thrives).

It has been put forward that life probably emerged and perished many times during the final formation of the earth, and that the ability to produce variation of form is the underpinning of "Adaptation".

Adaptation is not a planned function of any given organism, but the result of the organism's ability to live and reproduce in a given environment.

The next evolutionary force is said to be "Natural Selection". Once again, this is not a planned function of the organism, but a relatively random process, within the parameters of matter and energy transfer; of environmental situations, that adaptation provides as the motive force for those organismal variations best suited for a given environment to reproduce more frequently and therefore produce more variations that the nature of the environments more or less allows them to be selected to reproduce the next generation.

The main point of the above rhetoric is to emphasize that: from the Theory of Evolution point of view; that after the initial conditions that allowed life in the first place, there was no directional flow or design other than the determinant but not predestined parameters of the "Natural Laws" and/or initial conditions of the forming of the universe.

What ever creating force(s) that caused the universe, and all that followed are not processes that are tweaked or modified by "Outside" influences, but are sustained within the parameters of the above mentioned "Nature Laws" i.e., the various changes and exchanges between matter and energy (whether I fully understand them or not).

In other words, life is an emerging property of matter/energy exchanges and is in a symbiotic relationship with its environment.

Given the above, Biological Evolution is or can be envisioned as a limited process of matter/energy exchange, until the emerging properties of unconscious direction, a motive force, standing alone and operating within the organism, that somehow allows it to still be a product of matter/energy exchange, but to interact within itself (internal) and its environment (external) in a directed and adjustable manner to maintain the best balance of the two (internal vs external) venues.

This directed and adjustable function, while operating within the parameters of allowable matter/energy exchange ("Natural Laws") predicated a methodology that allowed weighted functions, within matters of degree of freedom, for the basic matters of life, from the general, to a detailed, more or less, cause and effect driven system that although not directed, was still able to monitor and adjust the internal venue in relationship to the external venue for the betterment of the organism.

In a sense, this could be viewed as a separation of the organism from its external environment, where by natural selection and/or adaptation was not wholly driven by the external environment, but due to the enclosing or "Closure" of the organism from the external environment, (more than just the physical membrane that separated the organism from it external environment). The organism itself took some control of its destiny by manipulating the environmental input in a more discrete and detailed manner.

This may have led to the simple organism being able to engulf another simple organism and live in symbiotic harmony and usher in the multiple cellular organism and nucleation of the genetic code and its processes and functions.

It follows that the multicellular event allowed for more complex organisms.

As this discourse is not on evolution, per se, but on why and how I think, I will jump to the development of the vertebrate lineages, where I perceive that the next (relative to this discourse) major set of emergent properties took place.

As an aside, an (this) emerging property may have been the pre-curser of vertebrates and the causal effect of their arrival?

In the above, I stated that the emergent property of unconscious direction gave the organism more control, I did not or do not intend to imply that the organism had any awareness of this function. There will be more on this "awareness", later.

At some point, (at the vertebrate (?) threshold) the emergent property of awareness must have expanded and manifested itself via a physical change in the organisms brain through a major or multiple mutational and/or copy error scenario.

Modern neural/cognitive science associates this higher order processing to the pre-frontal cortex, a (6) multilayered system of neural and supporting tissues.

Assuming, (given?) that the first pre-frontal cortex layer was mutation driven, it may have been the next step that allowed the genetic code, through an RNA/DNA copying effect, to string genetic material that duplicated the first layer in the pre-frontal cortex to such an extent that the many (6) layered present pre-frontal cortex evolved (more on this later).

But I am getting ahead of myself here, back to the first new, original layer.

Arbitrarily, I will assign a label to the emergent properties that we have described in my fantastic journey, thus far.

The emergent property of unconscious direction, I will call C1, and the emergent property, allowed/caused by the initial pre-frontal cortex layer, unconscious awareness, I will can C2.

It may be that C1 and C2 are both connected to genetic mutations leading to the pre-frontal cortex, but for the purposes of this discourse it is a detail (though very important) is not necessarily relevant to the thought flow of this scenario.

I am being very careful here to emphasize that C1 and C2 are subliminal functions of the internal venue of the organism. C1 first, a motivating force, within the organism, adjusting (if you will) the internals for maximum efficiency, without any connection to the external C2, unconscious awareness, on the other hand, operates (so to speak) external to the organism. Its awareness of the external venue (the environment) adds another layer of control to the organism, still at an unconscious level.

A note to the reader here:

Here and throughout this discourse, I do not advocate that any of the data/information that I present is these dichotomies are totally truthful or completely factual, but they are the basis for the premises that I operate on.

This is not the first nor the last time I will allude to this subject.

Another aside, the language I am using is in a backward context, that is, it must be viewed from the perception of now. I am now conscious, aware and have an embodied self representation ongoing, at all times, while in a wakeful state, and sometimes in a dream state, although symbologicly, they seem related.

Given the asides, while discussing C1 and C2, I am referring to a time in the organism's life when it was not conscious or consciously aware.

By definition, for the purposes of this discourse, I would like to add some more labels e.g., subconscious (C1), subconscious aware (C2) and super conscious (C...) i.e., consciousness, awareness and Self.

The labels may still be pretty arbitrary, vague and liquid for the reader, but if he or she has read this far, and is still reading, has probably been exposed to some of the concepts a priori, and has some idea of what I am trying to impart.

All of the above and some of the following are just the preamble to the dichotomy between Biological Evolution and Cultural Evolution. I only mention this so the reader doesn't loose sight (by the way, I am also the reader along with you) of the main goal of this part of the discourse on why and how I think as I do.

I am sorry about the first person business, but this is an introspective study of my "Self" and this presentation is a verbal representation that I am sharing with the reader, for what ever ego driven motive I have that forced me to make public my thoughts.

Back to it:

Next step, (C...) - through multiple emergent properties and various evolutional changes man (I) appeared on the scene with consciousness, awareness and self embodiment.

Somewhere during this transition, Biological Evolution was coupled with Cultural Evolution.

The rest of this portion (dichotomy) of the discourse will discuss my perspective (operating premise) of this transition and its effects and outcome.

I operate on the premise that the first "culture" appeared in the C2 phase as, in the vernacular, "instinct", that some time ago was housed in, and labeled "R", the reptilian or old brain.

What ever the case, the ramifications seem to me to have been personified in the schooling of fish and birds flocking and the early beginnings of sexual organism's parental care?

I know that the above is a big jump, but this discourse is not on evolution per se, so I leave the reader to fill in the details as they perceive them.

Again, for the purpose of this discourse, I will jump forward to the "homo" evolutionary line generally and the "Homo Sapiens" (I) line specifically.

But first, as an aside, at this point I will put forth my premise on the demise of Neanderthal Man.

As discussed above, the Pre-frontal Cortex seems to be the seat of Super Consciousness. Also, as stated above, this part of the brain, several (6) matted layers of neurons, one on top of the other, may have been the manifestation of a genetic abrasion that caused/ allowed mores copies of the genetic sequence that produced the first matted layer, resulted in the Pre-Frontal Cortex as it is today.

The point of this aside is that modern man, at some point, when the head size expansion, caused by the many (6) layers of the Pre-Frontal Cortex, had to stop when it reached the point where the female birth canal (the internal hip structure) did not expand to allow a larger head.

Again, seemly a function of Natural Selection/Adaptation, those organisms that had a mutational variation that cause the head to stop expanding i.e. stopped adding new layers to the Pre-Frontal Cortex i.e., terminated the "copy, copy the gene again" signal, survived to reproduce and carry on the line?

Back to Neanderthal man: fossil studies indicate that Neanderthal Man had a larger head than Homo Sapiens.

Perhaps the mutation that stopped the increase in Homo Sapiens' head size, didn't happen in Neanderthal Man, and as the head size increased, the female were unable to give birth, due to the limiting birth canal and the line became extinct.

This aside has or has not, factual value, even as a theory, but as this discourse is about how I think, I thought this would be a good example of my mental processes, Cause and Effect!

Also to make a life point, from one of my premises, what worked in the past will not always work and that things that didn't work still probably won't.

Thank you for your indulgence, if you're still with me? Now, on to Cultural Evolution and the ramifications and connection/ continuation of Biological Evolution.

Cultural Evolution operates on many levels that are sometimes associated with Biological Evolution, such as altruism.

Cultural Evolution seems mostly to be connected to social group, inter group or intra group activities.

Cultural Evolution has to do with the ability of the organism (homo) (I) to pass on learned/remembered material to the next generation, externally , and not through change or no changes in the genetic code, but thru example, symbols or vocally.

Homo:(man)(I)is/am a story teller, an it seems that even the internal processes of memory and recall are stored in the form of a story or a vignette.

Cultural Evolution transpires through a building up of traditions, those activities that aided survival and reproductive success relative to the band/group/tribe within a given geographical/environmental circumstance, possibly varying with the seasons.

The buildup of traditions and knowledge gleamed from nature and experience, passed on at first by example and verbally and later symbolically – the wall paintings and then the written word gave evolution a two pronged, entwined flow.

As a relevant aside, most species that have lived on earth in the last 3.5 billion years are extinct.

The estimated range is as much as 99.9% extinction.

The reason for these extinctions, other that catastrophe e.g., earth quakes, volcanoes or extra terrestrial bodies bombarding the earth, is attributed to the particular species being unable to survive in its particular environment, for what ever reason?

In a word, directionless natural selection and adaptation are not enough to insure reproductive success.

Although there is a continuum of organisms from the emergence of life so I can trace my ancestry (so to speak) to the original life form(s), the majority (99.9%) of the variations of that (those) life forms are no longer with us.

I presented this aside to emphasize the difference between non-directional changes, (Biological Evolution) and directional change (or stability) through Cultural Evolution.

Homo (I) am/is the first species that can live anywhere on earth, by directional adaptation (Cultural Evolution), rather than non-directional (Biological Evolution).

What I am trying to get at, is that Cultural Evolution, driven in part by the ability to remember the past and predict the future, is a situational problem solving apparatus that increase in breadth and width, through time, by being able to manipulate parties involved; both physical beings and the environment.

Cultural Evolution is, in essence, the measure of control Homo (I) has/have taken out of natures hand and placed it in my own.

In conclusion, Cultural Evolution has allowed Homo (I) to more or less override the process of natural selection an adaptation (Biological Evolution) and put us/it in stasis.

By definition, stasis is the function of a species to remain the same, evolution wise, with only minor variation, for long periods of time and not go extinct during that stasis period.

Being able to remember and learn from our mistakes and pass this knowledge on to the next generation is the driving for of Cultural Evolution.

The Blank Slate and Human Nature

The Blank Slate and Human Nature Dichotomy is the third facet of the Evolution/Heredity, Nature/Nurture, Blank Slate/Human Nature Trichotomy, a Polychotomy, if your will.

From the Blank Slate point of view, the organism (Homo) (I) are/is born with the "R", that reptilian brain system, consisting only of the tools for living and breathing, and a few basic instincts, as to suckle, to cry when hurt or hungry/thirsty and not much else.

From the Blank Slate point of view, all else is mimicked, conditioned or learned through the life experience.

And, after the basic design is laid down and operated upon up to birth, everything else is environmentally driven.

In the face of current levels of research and understanding about the brain/mind situation, the Blank Slate advocates have conceded that speech is also part of the basic "instincts", but that is about the limit of their concession to any innate "Human Nature".

A very limited point of view; allowing for little more than a few basic capabilities, without the outside environmental input.

Human Nature advocates, on the other hand, operate from a much more varied and complex palate, so to speak.

The Blank Slate paradigm, while encompassing the "R" factor as a neural basis of the living process, and embracing the Nurture side of Nature/Nurture, emphasizes the post natal environment/experience and the ramifications of same.

Given that the organism in question, (Homo)(I) had/have/has a viable and complete (average?) gamete stage, from the Human Nature point of view, all other processes, functions, growth; etc. etc. are based on the genetic propensities of the organism, tempered with the whole of the Nature/Nurture dichotomy.

This is a very dense proposition, so several dozens of volumes have been dedicated to the various aspects of it in massive detail. For the purpose of this discourse, I will try to keep brevet and simple; by example, that the reader can extrapolate from their knowledge base and inclination (How They Think, the reason for this discourse in the first place i.e., How do I Think).

In the overall process; there is, from the point of view of the Human Nature advocates, both fixed and variable capabilities and limitations in the individual organism (Homo)/(I).

I will partially list some of the fixed functions or sub-organs:

(1) eye color, (2) range of the senses (basic) i.e., each individual has the ability to hear certain frequencies, smell certain things and see certain colors and shades of colors, (3) Basic skeletal design e.g., height, facial features, ears, foot size and basic dexterity, (4) for what ever genetic reason, talents and temperament seem to be fixed within a more controlled set of parameters than the variable traits that I will discuss below.

The variability of functions or sub-organs is virtually unlimited. The reader will have to extrapolate more in this phase than the above.

I will try; in a simple manner, still with content and brevity, to delineate the variables laid down or overlaid, in a temporal sequence from the gamete stage.

Here the previous discussion on Nurture is a given, with the following enhancements and possible redundancies.

Given the basic gamete potential (understandably a range), any lack of the necessary nutrients or basic care can curtail this potential in many ways.

Assuming that the nutrient and care functions are covered through the birth stage i.e., the organism is average at birth. At this point the Blank Slate point of view is relevant: though still limited; the organism learns by operating with the external world (Environment).

But, here is where the Blank Slate and Human Nature advocates begin to part ways.

Given the basic genetic makeup and the skeletal variations, what the organism picks up and operates on is internally driven and not externally driven.

The environment can expose the organism (or even fail to expose), but the makeup of the organism controls the acceptance or disregard of the exposure.

Even though the Blank Slate advocates have given away to the idea that the speech capabilities are part of Human Nature, they are still driven (?) to operate on the premise that it's just an aside that allows communication and is not a sign post that points to a various array of other facets of Human Nature or the variation of these facets of Human Nature.

This is where the genetic (Hereditary) side and the Environmental side of the organism development and continuity come into conflict; from the points of view of the Blank Slate proponents and those who advocate Human Nature as the driving (though not predestined) force.

As stated above, the first external (to the organism) or environmental influence is (for the purpose of this discourse), nurture i.e., the mothers, after gamete, input to the organism.

If the mother is healthy, has a good diet and doesn't do toxic drugs (a slippery variable today), the maximum potential of the genetic capabilities and limitations are most probably present.

A super healthy mother on a super appropriate diet may give the organism some advantage; but, for my purpose, in this discourse, it may be best to assume an average mother in good health, on a good clean diet.

Using the infant studies over the last century as a basis, it seems apparent that (A) there is a common (average/mean) learning curve for young organisms, and (B) that that learning curve can be raised or lowered by the external stimulation given the organism e.g., mobiles, music, singing, swimming lessons, bright colors, conversation, games, attention and affection (among others that I may not even be aware of?).

This being the case, by definition, I operate on the premise that the better (?) the initial external stimulational environment, the more of the organism's potentials will have a chance to be achieved.

After the initial infant state, and into the toddler stage, the parents native language is learned, along with the variations of the capabilities and limitations of said parents e.g., education, social status, biases, prejudices, and most of all (perhaps?), the level of care giving (probably a sliding scale of ranges that may or may not be advantageous to the new organism).

In the formative years i.e., 3 to 5 years, it has been said that the basic right and wrong and primary minimum social skill are set.

Given the above as a working hypothesis, it seems that the Blank Slate premise is not working alone.

Although much of the above points toward the external/environmental inputs, the ability of the organism to take advantage of these inputs is basically a function of the capabilities and limitations of the organism derived from it's genetic code.

By/for example, let's go back to the stimulations that were discussed:

(A) Mobiles... The ability to see and realize the special attributes of mobiles may be a common factor in why the ability to recall, imagine and manipulate the internal, representations is extremely varied from individual to individual.

(B) Music... Though universally (thought to be) soothing and stimulating, and capable of inspiring emotion, the capabilities and limitations of each organism's auditory system (ears?) has a certain variation of frequency appreciation, and some internal (talent, if you will) function that allows some organisms to appreciate the music more, and again the capabilities and limitations of recalled/remembered representations and internal manipulation of same.

(C) Singing... Singing has dual input, both visual and auditory, and the same attributes of music apply, with the added visual capabilities and limitations of the range of light frequencies available to the organism.

(D) Swimming... New organism (babies) seem to have a propensity to swim (a carryover from the womb environment?), but the skeletal makeup of the individual organism will be the deciding factor of how efficient a swimmer the organism turns out.

(E) Bright Colors... In infant studies, it appears that later (toddler onward) color appreciation and variation potential is enhanced in those organisms that were exposed to more bright colors in the infant stage.

This; however, is again modulated by the capabilities and limitations of the visual frequency range of the concerned organism.

As an aside, the female color ranges seem to be broader than male, and some individuals are able to visualize the color spectrum beyond the normal (average) range, understanding that the human eye is limited to what light wave frequencies it can accommodate.

I could go on thru the list, but the same factors would still come up in a needless redundant manner.

What attributes of the environmental input that the organism can process and use (and therefore recall and reuse) depends entirely on the capabilities and limitations of the organism internal (genetic, biological) processes.

That the organism is totally driven by genetic propensities or that culture and conditioning control the organism are both over statements, but the given organisms output, outlook or result (if you will), will only be allowed by the capabilities and limitations of the internal processes of the organism, although they be may modified by external influences.

If you, the reader, doubt this, ask yourself why good people have bad children and bad people have good children and average people have good and bad children. Most of all, why do twins (genetic clones), raised in different environments have so many personality traits in conjunction, (twin studies over the last century, have time and time again come to this same result, barring brain damage in one of the subjects).

There is probably not a gene for every personality facet, but the chances are that the various admixtures of several genetic operations direct a potential behavior, that can be enhanced or inhibited by environmental input, but not always.

I operate on the premise that the I that this discourse is about, is a very complicated mixture of a genetic base with environmental/cultural modifications.

Science and Theology

Science is basically the observation and study of nature.

As nature is the subject of science, a primary function of science is to look for and analyze "Natural Laws".

Laws, by their very nature, are systems with beginnings and ends (for the most part).

That being the case, cause (beginnings) and effects (ends) are the milestones of science.

At this point in history, there seems to be two levels (but not separate?) or sets of laws, the laws of "Classical Physics" and the laws of "Quantum Physics" or the laws of the macro and micro aspects of the universe (to be discussed in more detail in another section of this discourse).

Overall, from the scientific point of view, laws have fixed rules; though sometimes hard to discern, that cannot be, and are not broken.

At the most esoteric levels of science there is another dichotomy, a universe without a beginning, that has always existed, and in some manner, will always exist vs/or a universe that had a beginning i.e., the "Big Bang".

In the case of the always universe, the scientists that advocate this seem to have alleviated/eliminated the need for cause or a creative force (in the vernacular, GOD).

As an aside, the premise I operate on, as I have stated before, and will state again and again, is, as I am finite and the universal data base (from my point of view) is infinite, not only can I not have enough data to discern the "Truth", and therefore not believe or disbelieve anything, and must, to survive, operate on various premises, based on the data that I do have (that I perceive), operate on a cause and effect premise i.e., there is a beginning of things.

Back to the main stream: In the case of the "Big Bang" universe, by definition, there was/is a creative force, unknown and probably unknowable, that initiated the universal laws, set the initial/starting conditions for the singularity that preceded the big bang and then left the building.

This science (religion?) is called Deism.

This is where science and theology part ways.

The theologists, by definition, operate on the premise that the creative force (in the vernacular, GOD), did not leave the building, but is here now and interacts with the creation.

Theology and Religion

Theology is the methodology that theists use to explain their operating premise that the creative force (in the vernacular GOD), besides being the creator of the universe, has remained involved with the structures and organisms of the universe.

Religion, on the other hand, with its many facets, the codification of morals and ethics, prayers and allusions to punishments e.g., Limbo, Purgatory and/or Hell, live by, and for the most part assume that they and only they have a pipeline to GOD.

The dichotomy between the two is relatively simple, theists operate on the premise of and interactive GOD and religion assumes the role of deciding what GOD wants humanity to do, and what GOD will do to those that don't obey those religious tenets.

Natural Selection and Adaptation

This is another dichotomy, one of many, in this discourse, that is covered in another dichotomy and therefore may seem overly redundant.

I do it in this manner to try to emphasize that there may be some root heuristics and/or algorithms (if you will), that come up over and over in my thinking process.

Also, Natural Selection and Adaptation are a basic tenet of Darwinism Evolution and are also relevant in any (many?) systems and/or enterprises, but not always correctly understood, from my point of view, because they are not predestined, as some people assume, but are non-directional.

My favorite and most valuable tool in the Super Conscious/ Cognitive phase of my thinking process is the dialectic – thesis, antithesis and synthesis.

This is the very essence of the change (evolution) process, in that, as I compromise, I naturally select the best option and adapt the synthesis to accommodate it.

Although I understand the difference between the directionless of Natural Selection and Adaptation in biological Evolution (more about this later?), and the directed (Super Conscious vs unconscious) cognitive process, the basic idea is the same, things that work in a given situation will be selected as part of scenario for future same situational solutions.

With that overview of this specific situation and the understanding that there will be many incidents of duplication and redundancy throughout this discourse for basically the same reason, I will now try to get back to the point.

Natural Selection and Adaptation were first joined by Darwin as a/the basis for his theory of evolution.

In camera, and very simply (I hope not simplistically), I will try to cover the concept, (in order to show the value of the concept to my thinking process).

Organisms vary from generation to generation.

Asexual organisms vary due to DNA/RNA copying errors and/or toxic external (environmental) causes e.g., pollutants and/or various radioactive or cosmic particle interactions.

Sexual organisms vary due to the mixing of the genetic code (meiosis) and also the same causes as the asexual organisms.

The organisms born with these variations live or die according to their adaptation to the environment (not their ability to adapt,but the ability to live and reproduce in that given environment [niche]).

If an organism lives in an environment (niche) slightly different than its parents and reproduces future generations, it is said to be Naturally Selected.

As an aside, but relevant, this is the front end of the new specie function and a future generation of variation, and another cycle of Natural Selection and Adaptation, that may have led the simple, single celled organisms to the complex, multicellular organisms that are now present (I).

This Natural Selection and Adaptation is not confined to the bio-evolutional world, but also applies to tradition, culture, technology, science, business and living in general, a basic function of all facets of life.

Republic and Democracy

I perceive that early on, bands and tribes consisted of people who were very alike traditionally and culturally and didn't warrant much more than a communal system of government, with possibly a hierarchal male and/or female, or both, leader e.g., hunter/gathers.

At the dawn of civilization, (city dwelling), a new system became necessary, mainly due to the merging of groups with different traditions and/or cultures.

Cities were probably, at the beginning, controlled by a founding group, with a strong leader; but, as the cities grew into city-states and the diverse groups that joined the city or were absorbed by the city, each groups traditional and/or cultural nature were either suppressed by force and channeled into the power groups ways or enclaves (quarters?) of mutually respected areas of the cities were established and some system of cooperation arranged?

In a word, there were probably ethnic neighborhoods that produced diverse goods and services that may have been distributed to and from a central market place.

At some point, as the city grew in complexity, there was bound to be strife?

I think the term "civilization", entails a method or methods of suppressing this strife and living in harmony.

Given the above preamble, for what ever it's worth, factually or historical wise, I have arrived at the theme of this dichotomy i.e., Republic and Democracy.

I will operate on the premise that democracies came first as an out growth of the strong man system.

As villages/towns grew in to cities, and diverse groups came together, each with their own strong man, some system of cooperation, liken to our city councils, must have come into being.

This council, thru a simple majority vote, laid down the basic operating procedures (laws) of the city.

By definition: a multicultural governmental system controlled by a simple majority vote is called a democracy, vs a strong man system, called sovereignty, and ruled by force, rather than cooperation.

Somewhere along the line, the cities became integrated enough that the ethnic strong man, neighborhood system's impact lessoned, and the vote, if you will, was delegated downward to all free men (understanding, that in this phase of civilization there were slaves, who had little or no input).

This system of all free men still ruled by simple majority, thru their elected representatives, a council of the people, democracy was born.

As often happens as systems become more complex, diverse forces emerge that are not compatible with the status quo.

In the case of civilizations, there came a point where there were too many points of view; a multicultural society with strong enclaves, too complex for a simple majority rules system to work.

Each power enclave had to be served in some manner.

Hence the republic was born, and turned the wheel back to where a representative body was elected by all free men in each enclave (liken to the simple neighborhood councils of the past), so that each facet of the population and their point of view was served.

It is good to note here that this is circular system i.e., strongman to strongmen to free men simple majority, Morphing into cooperation.

I will continue this circle by exploring the rise and fall of other political systems, in other dichotomies.

A final aside for this dichotomy:

Please understand and try to see; even through my deviation and digressions may make it hard, that my main thrust of this discourse is to analyze and find out how and why I think as I do, but not necessarily what I think..

Democrat and Republican

When I think of Democrat and Republican, I think of only the American political system.

My first position is/was very juvenile/sophomoric.

You elect a Democrat and then the voters tell him/her what to do.

You elect a Republican and he/she (the elitist) does what is best for you.

At the current stage/level/phase of our political system, that is too simplistic because both parties now have contingency pressures, due to the increase of Multi-Culturism?

My next level of thought; therefore, follows the conservative (right wing) and the liberal (left wing) political philosophies.

These seem at times to be at extremes, as that in most other things, compromise (The Dialectic) seems to be the order of the day?

At the present time; however, we seem to be at a point of a near 50/50 split on the voting for what ever major party, Democratic or Republican, and the motivation behind the voting, though still encumbered with the extreme left/right factions, seem to swing on the moderate/independent sector.

This seems to me to be the real culmination of my premise on the civilized (multicultural City/States), republican system i.e., although still with the principle of the majority rule, there is a many leveled hierarchal operation, where many separate majority blocks are wielding or possessing the power to fulfill the republic scenario – something for every sector of the multicultural public realm, with a leaning toward the moderate conservative.

The unique part of this outcome or present state of affairs does not seem to advocate the republic system; but, more or less screams, democracy, global democracy, and democracy for all.

So it seems to me to boil down to a system, or perceived or wished for system, that what matters is that each individual is allowed input, with result, into the system, and any elected body speaks with the will of the people across all their various needs and wants.

Is a global; life, liberty and the pursuit of happiness in our future and is the two party system, Democratic and Republican, morphing into, an across the board representation that will finally fulfill the idea for "A Republic"?

Liberal – Moderate – Conservative

Although Liberal, Moderate & Conservative political philosophies may have relatively similar connotations worldwide, I think of them mostly as a local American phenomenon.

As an individual, I am partial to all three, although not in the same situations e.g., Liberal civil rights, moderate regulation, and conservative legal/judicial, to cover the spectrum with a broad brush.

But the overall meaning of the terms has to do with the results of the politics that support and/or follow them.

It seems evident to me (my operational premise), that liberal politics lead to a welfare state, bigger government, higher taxes, less choice i.e., more regulation and a more or less pseudo redistribution of the wealth to reach, in theory, a more level playing field?

If taken to extremes, to socialism–Communism (a totalitarian proletariat government) or to social-fascism (a completely totalitarian malignant State), neither which seem to work in the long run, due to their need carry out their doctrine outside their borders, and sooner or later be thwarted by their neighbors.

As an aside, all political and religious systems seem to want to share their philosophies with others, either forcefully or not. Some times it works, but there is almost always some resistance from the established belief systems of their neighbors.

Moderation (at least, in the American system) seems to be to be a buffer between the elements of the Republican (Conservative) and the Democratic (Liberal) parties.

It is a middle ground situation that allows compromise that overrides the metaphor that any three parties can't agree on anything.

Parties A/B (Liberal/Moderate) enacts some legislation by merging their vote to get a majority.

Parties B/C (Moderates/Conservatives) the same with other issues, and sometimes a Bi-partisan (A/C) situation arises.

What this seems to be saying is that the Moderate voting block, by its very nature, is the corner stone of a (our?) republic?

Conservative points of view, on the third hand, seem to (wish/imply/promote) the power of the individual to be responsible for their on fate and action, smaller government, less regulation, laissez faire economics, less communal endeavors and increased personal freedoms, tempered by a harsh judicial that punishes those who do not follow the restraints of the small, but not ineffectual, rule setting government.

This point of view, also carried to extremes, can lead to the plutocratic and/or Totalitarian, a police state, because of a seeming facet of human nature; that, while individualism is great, if carried to extremes, it must be extremely policed.

What the above says, is that political postures, without a moderating force can and often and usually do, revert back to the strong man (or council) type of rule that pre-dated working civilizations?

I must make the point here again, that none of the above may be truthful in fact or theory, but as this discourse is an analysis of how I think, these are part of the premises that I operate from.

Yin and Yang

In my normal thought process Yin and Yang are the female and male aspect of human nature.

This in itself, is defining women and men as "different" – a true dichotomy.

But; on the other hand, while researching the basis for my thought process, I researched the basis on Yin and Yang and found that they are not just a dichotomy, but the very epitome of the dialectic, at its most dynamic.

The basis of Yin and Yang is found in ancient Chinese Taoist philosophy, which expresses mono/dual, singular/plural in everything in nature and ourselves.

The Yin involves the singularity and unitary aspects of us and the universe, while the Yang expresses the diversity and dualism.

The prominent factor, for the purposes of this discourse, is to add a layer of dynamic range to the (my) thinking process.

The Ying and Yang are ever pulling at each other and are always in flux.

This leads to the fluid/liquid/ambivalent states of my operating premises in different situations, circumstance and context, and my various range of moods and emotional states, connected back to traumatic events that highlight aspects of recall, and colors decisions.

Local and Global (1)

Local and Global concepts and functions are a complex array within the concept of my thinking process.

They are liken to Russian Dolls that fit within each other, in that the whole package may be classified as Global and any combination of those within can be considered Local and/or Global.

Local and Global are, in this sense, also associated with fractal phenomena.

There is a certain similarity between the fractals and the whole, as there is between Local and Global, but the highlights and peaks of the fractals are smoothed some in the whole or Global situation.

There is at once a dichotomy/dialectic operation involved.

Where ever I turn, I find that there is a propensity for compromise and cooperation in every nuance of my thinking process, a weighted, fuzzy internal process that solidifies into a solution.

Each dichotomy blends itself into a workable whole that is/are single pixels, particles or threads in the fabric of the conscious/cogent functions that back up my thinking process.

With all this going on, do I still have free will?

Local and Global (2)

This Local and Global dichotomy is another set of Russian Dolls, in that depending on the time and distance, for instance, their meaning can change faces.

Within the Solar System, the Earth is local, the Solar System Global, but within the Galaxy the Solar System is local.

I only mean that at the ends of the spectrum, to reemphasize the point that word/concept meanings are not static or absolute, but have to be operated on in reference to their context or situations, temporal or spatial.

As I get deeper into this discourse on dichotomies, I run into this often, and may allude to it in those dichotomies that seem to apply more than others.

But, as usual I digress.

A situation/scenario is local, under normal circumstances if the event(s) are contained within certain parameters, and Global if many of them, while individual, have connecting attributes e.g., basketball tournaments, city sectional, regional, and State.

The value of operating from a local perspective is analogous to the reduction operation in science.

One may be able to observe and study a small area (local) in great detail and make assumptions about a large area (Global) – Induction?

From the point of view of how I gather data and/or experience about subjects/objects, to use in the thinking process, the local/global dichotomy is or seems to be, a short cut allowing faster (less energy consuming) decisions, keeping in mind the limitation of the duration of short term memory and rapidly changing environmental (external) situations.

Once again I am back to the Pleistocene, "R" based survival functions.

Every facet of my current thinking process seems to be based on this foundation i.e., does or does not this decision enhance my survival potential.

I realize that this seems far a field from a simple dichotomy of Local/Global; but, tongue in cheek, that is the reality of the Russian Doll of Global vs Local, and as stated above, perhaps the very threads of the tapestry of my thought process, as a whole.

The analogy between a tapestry and a neural network comes to mind.

RNA Mutation
(copy errors) and DNA Mutation
(environmental causes)

In biological evolution, there are tenants such as Variation, Natural Selection and Adaptation.

This Dichotomy will explore some of what's behind these concepts and/or functions.

First, a basic primer: All living organisms (asexual and/or sexual) are reproduced by a duplication process.

In single cell organisms, the parent cell develops a copy of it self and then splits in two, into two daughter cells.

In multicellular organisms, the female produces and egg and the males produce a sperm, they merge and produce a new organism. In asexual organisms, the female fulfills both functions.

For my purposes, in this discourse, by definition, I will analyze the multicellular sexual organisms.

The underlying system that drives this reproduction cycle is the cellular nucleolus and other internals.

My purpose with this dichotomy is to isolate and define the reasons behind variation, natural selection, and adaptation and their relation to each other.

This is not going to be a deep, detailed biological survey of cellular functions, but simplified at the duplication (if you will) process.

The DNA is a double helix that carries two copies of the organisms' genome.

The RNA initiates a process that unwinds the helix and copies (and/or duplicates) one half of the helix, that ultimately end up merged with the half helix from the other partner, into a gamete.

This is a weak and very general explanation of the process, but the reader will have to fill in the blanks from their internal knowledge or gleam it from other parts of this discourse, because the dichotomy is limited not to cover the whole process, but to investigate the reasons behind failure of the copying or duplication process to be perfect.

With out all the bells and whistles that make up the organelles in the cell, I will limit this discourse to the copying process of the RNA and the status or situation of the RNA copy.

As an aside, I am operating here only on the germ sells (egg and sperm), as the only traits of the organism that are carried forward to the new generation, comes from them.

The reason that this is important is that only the mutations or damages in the germ cell are carried forward to the next generation.

To begin, it has to be understood that the DNA bases are chemical compounds (mini-molecules) and are subject to environmental situations.

They can be influenced and or slightly changed by toxins and/or cosmic or other radiation.

Secondly, the RNA copying process must utilize the resources available to produce the new duplicated compounds (bases).

If the DNA helix bases have been altered (mutated) the mutated base will be copied. I call this a DNA mutation error.

If during the copying process the RNA has to substitute a less perfect resource into a base, this can cause an RNA copying error. Also environmental situations can add to the error syndrome.

After the merging of the egg and sperm and the copying sequence, the meiosis process merges the male and female halves of the helix from each partner into a single set of chromosomes.

The entire process, within a range of no errors to many errors, is the root of the variation from one generation to the next.

The result of this range of error's, is minor to major variation and in extreme cases the death or abortion of a particular gamete or fetus.

It must be understood that those gametes or fetus that survive have variations that are severally constrained by the structural functions of the new organism.

Except in rare (and mostly only in theory) cases, the variations are limited to enhanced mobility, increased ability to utilize (transfer) recourses from the external environment and increased/decreased tolerance of environmental situations.

This is where natural selection and adaptation come into play.

If the new variation is able to survive (adapt, without volition) in a environmental niche that was not compatible with the parent organism, the new organism is said to be naturally selected to thrive and reproduce the next generation.

I know the above is thin and full of holes, but once again, as this entire discourse is about how and why I think as I do; the biological details are not the driving force, but just part of the general information/data flow.

Each of these thin, but overlapping dichotomies, I hope, will weave a full tapestry that is the base of my thinking processes and the premises that I operate from.

To Reason and to Rationalize

In a goal oriented thought process or any search for a solution, either in science of just planning a vacation, I reason or rationalize to come to a conclusion.

There are merits to both systems, depending on the type of search.

In both instances, alone the path to the correct or required/desired results, there are pertinent data points.

Basically, when I rationalize, I choose those data points to work with that lead me to my preconceived goal.

On the other hand, as in unbiased scientific research, I follow all the data points to the end, if the preconceived goal is reached or not.

Depending on the underlying motivations of the search, either method may give the result of that motivation?

One often rationalizes in interpersonal relationships, where the data points   that drive the other party or parties are unknown, and also in intrapersonal relationships, where the implicit data points are not in conscious awareness, when one is trying to fool ones self. This is the only way it can be done and in the long run the only time I should rationalize.

In all other cases, I should reason through to the solution.

Systematic or Emergent

Within systems in general, and living organism specifically, two functions direct outcomes.

The first is based on the "Natural Laws", which define the Capabilities and Limitations of a given set of ingredients to interact.

The second, the Emergent Property, is an added value. In the vernacular, it is the gestalt result of the end being more than the sum of its parts.

The above descriptions is based on my understanding of present knowledge, and gives the intuitive feeling that the life force is an Emergent Property that comes from without, which is probably a strong basis for theism and religious thought.

I have no argument with this; however, being a deist, I operate under the premise that the Creative Force (The Absolute Unknowable) initiated the "Natural Laws" and set the initial/starting conditions of the universe, part of which was the ability of some systems to produce/exhibit more than the sum of their parts.

This is the "Magic" of life: the thought process of the more gifted members of humanity; to achieve some preconceived, determinate, but not predestined goals, of the Creative Force, caused(?) when the initial/staring conditions were set?

Conscious, Super Conscious and Unconscious

While perusing the "popular" literature on neural science, neural psychology, neural physiology, consciousness, etc, - dozens of volumes, I find a veritable polychotomy of description, levels, names, divisions, ranges, etc, of the mind/brain/body phenomena.

As this discourse is mostly a series of dichotomies, I have reduced this one on consciousness/awareness/wakefulness to two categories.

Two conscious states: the unconscious operating below the super conscious.

I know this reduction merges, fades and leaves out much detail, but once again I emphasize that this discourse is on how and why I think like I do, and while I follow the various theoretical discussions in the many volumes, as I read them, their lack of semantic closure of the language and terms used, it just fades away into the reduced area that I am addressing here?

The Subconscious realm is 80% of the picture; by definition, from the 80/20 syndrome. It involves basic autonomous body functions, the visceral e.g., bones, blood, muscle and other body tissues, the vital and various hormonal systems, the brain and nervous system itself and all their functions combined with the input from the senses and the interaction with "R", the reptilian neural package that houses our basic pre-mammal instincts, and last but not least, the most basic of all, and the underlying basis of our being, the genetic system, and the functions that turns genes on and off to produce the various enzymes, catalysts, proteins, and what ever, that are needed during various phases of our daily life.

This part of my "Operating System", in a computer analogy that seems common in the literature, operates in the back round i.e., they are unconscious functions.

Although I am awake, I am not conscious (aware) of these activities in the normal and prevalent case.

On again, in computereze, they are the operating platform for the super conscious.

As the instinctive subconscious is the realm of "R" and related systems, the Super Conscious seem to be housed in the pre-frontal cortex, who's layers (6) of neuron sheets in the brain that were (or seem to have been) grown in conjunction with the improvement of the mammalian cognitive process?

If either the cognitive dexterity improvement drove the building of the new neural layers in the pre-frontal cortex or the build up of the layers drove cognizance and dexterity may never be known, but they are both now present and the driving force behind the Super Conscious states.

Under normal circumstances; discounting deep meditation and bio-feedback functions in some of the new theories and procedures, the Super Conscious (Self, if you will) is not aware of the sub conscious, although all the external data that drives the Super Conscious is filtered through and furnished by the sub conscious.

The cognitive systems operate as if they are using external senses data only and do not formally recognize that the actual thought processes or a mixing of current real time data merged with stored experience, memories and representations and then sent up to the Super Conscious for further real time processing.

I hope that I haven't lost the reader here; but, I went through all of this in this manner to emphasize that how and why I think as I do is based first on the basic evolutionary back round of my processes before birth, and then added too and modified by my life experiences, data input, retention and various and sundry environmental exposures.

Once again, in computereze, I am an evolutional operating system, pre-programmed to operate on externally supplied data bases, with modifications possible to the operating system?

Genetic (Cognitive)
and Genetic (intuitive)

In the Genetic (Cognitive) and Genetic (Intuitive) dichotomy, I am going to try (am trying) at two levels, sometimes?

Starting with the Genetic (Intuitive), I peruse the nature side of the organisms' growth.

The genetic code generates (or directs) the growth of the fetus through the body/brain phases.

The body is important because it is the reservoir, so to speak, where much external data collect prior to its use by the central nervous system and brain functions.

For my purposes, on the Genetic (intuitive) side, I focus on "R" or the pre-mammalian center, where, what I call my intuitions and/or a basic part of the unconscious resides.

Also part of the genetic side here, in that this and related areas of the brain also control the activation/deactivation of certain genes to fulfill certain functions during the daily/monthly/annual etc. cycles of life e.g., when birds build nests, bees hive and mammals menses.

The Genetic (Cognitive) side, while underpinned by the Genetic (intuitive) side and also built/grown/directed by the genes during the fetal period, is mainly centered in the frontal brain, basically in the pre-frontal cortex.

As previously alluded to, this area, multiple (6) layers of neural mats were laid over the "R" , mid brain, brain stem, back bone and general nervous system some time starting, probably, pre-mammalian?

As the mammals became larger and more complex, some mutation or copying error allowed more neural mats to be generated and overlaid in/on the pre-frontal cortex, increasing the size of the brain and head of the organism. I am assuming that some where/time during the primate stages and culminating at the top or Homo stage (so to speak), and then this genetic function that allowed the multiple copies ceased to function (for whatever organism variational reason), when the organisms head size was limited by the birth channel structure in the female hip.

This redundancy is an aside, relevant to the whole discourse, not especially to this dichotomy, which is primarily interested in the function of said Pre-frontal cortex.

All the machinery necessary for life and survival are located in "R", but for my purposes defined as subconscious.

My next step (level) of interest is the Super Conscious, understanding the Trichotomy of consciousness based on first being aware/awake (so to speak) and conscious leads to the dichotomy of the Sub Conscious, previously described, and the Super Consciousness, the generation and maintaining the "Self".

This Super Consciousness, "Self Awareness", is an emerging property allowed/generated by the neural networks in the pre-frontal cortex, in conjunction with "R" and the data from external sources, coupled with "remembered" representations of past experience cycles of "R" and externals, managed by the built in Capabilities and Limitations (hard wired, to use more computerize) into the evolved living operating systems.

In other words, although much of who and what I am and how and why I think as I do is based on the experience from external and feedback looped with previous experiences, this is only data or data bases that are controlled by a priori (though malleable) propensities controlled by said Capabilities and Limitations of the system with cooperation of the emerging properties (the real magic of the live cycle).

Once again, I know this is muddy: this reduced presentation is the basis for the basic premises that I operate from.

Inevitable and Truly Random

Inevitable and Truly Random meet only a few times in their functional duration: that is they are not always a dichotomy and mostly are mutually exclusive or stand alone.

For my purposes here, the dichotomy is related to a facet of pre-destiny.

In an instance where they are syntactically and grammatically connected they are truly a dichotomy.

In one sense, Truly Random can be associated with chaos, but at the same time, within a chaotic situation it is inevitable that an emerging property that has been labeled "Special Attractor" happens.

On the other hand, the origin of life is heralded as Truly Random phenomena, while death is inevitable.

Well, enough said; but, my purpose for using the dichotomy in this discourse is not limited to the above, and not really concerned with those areas, but is concerned with processes (such as cognition and action) that are constituted of a stream of truly random, within deterministic, but not predestined parameters that lead to an inevitable conclusion or act, given the input data and feedback from internal representations.

My point, though nebulous and even fuzzy to me, is that my thought/thinking process (the many times eluded for reason for this discourse) starts with the truly random events on many levels internal and external to the organism, and inevitably lead to a decision – the right one allowing the organism to survive for the static discrete moment, while the wrong on may terminate the organisms existence immediately, or at a later static discrete moment that will have been mediated by that or a collection of other bad decisions.

The connection with the first part of this dichotomy is, although the inputs of existence are truly random and the end (death of the organism) is inevitable, the important part of this scenario is that part of the process that sustains the life force.

While the organism lives, it is responsible, either sub-consciously or consciously for its' own acts and existence, within the bounds of free will.

I am not sure that the above will be relevant to the reader, but it does give me another overlapping, redundant, serial, parallel, distributed, insight into how and why I think as I do.

Emotion and Logic

Once again, Emotion and Logic are not always in a dichotomic state, but when they are, they may be driven by one another in a dialectic manner?

Emotions generated by "R", cause/allow special feelings in response to various visceral processes combined with external neural inputs, and are a key factor in an organism's overt activities, but their outcome, when related to an act of body or thought are modified by the Super-Conscious logic of the situation, unless the organism is psychotic.

This loop represents a basic survival strategy of the higher level cognitive organism.

If the psychosis overrides the logical of the given situation, the organism is put in jeopardy.

This is another facet of the function of the nebulous "Free Will".

During my thinking process, am I truly responsible for my own act or even in control?

If this question is not rectified early on in the organism's life cycle and maintained there after, many of the available psychosis within the organism will destroy it.

In order to survive, I must control the Beast within.

Philosophical and Esthetic

I see this dichotomy between the love of learning, alone with the various views of the values of what is learned and their ramifications, and the love of beauty: viewed, heard, smelled or tactilely felt.

In a word, what is the relationship between the reviewing of stored internal representations of philosophy (deep, retrospective thinking) and the real time stimulations of beauty on the organism?

Is there a compartmentalized, modular, set of brain structures and their various sets of feed back apparatus that differentiate between philosophy and esthetics or do they feed on one another?

The real question here, is can I, the thinker, separate the difference between the high logic of philosophical reasoning and the emotional power of the beauty of the moment, from what ever source?

Do I have "Free Will", through a refined evolutionary driven cognitive system, or am I a victim of whim and caprice, and what are the defining, deterministic, but not predestined parameters involved?

In a word, am I in control and therefore responsible for my own actions or just a twig driven by the universal wind?

Talkers/Readers/Loners
and Doers/Active Joiners

I perceive that there are many types of people in this world, but they mostly fall into two groups, the introverted, who mostly talk it, read about it and stay somewhat isolated, and in a more or less observing mode, with maybe some involvement in major things, such a presidential election, and if and when they socialize, inter actions are really intra actions. It really is only about us, (I'm one).

On the other hand, the extrovert or the doers, activists and joiners, while they may observe the world, its usually (or it seems to be) from a pretty narrow perspective; but, beside actively doing, they also join with others with relatively the same point of view, then exercise great powers, and are the movers and shakers of the world, as a general trend and in seemingly most cases?

However, there is some evidence, that in many pivotal points in history and/or cultural evolution, it was/is the introverted loner, reader and talker that input the impedance that caused/allowed and/or directed the change.

The point is, my thinking process, however it varies, has a place in the pecking (social) order!

Sexual Reproduction and Asexual/Sexual Reproduction

On of the first emotions I remember was pride, but of not being proud, but of having my pride hurt.

Hurt feelings were (are) a biggie.

Until I was introduced to Greek Mythology I had not heard of Hubris; that is, false pride.

Looking back from that point, I found that many incidents of hurt feelings, though associated with hurt pride, the pride that was hurt was not based on reality, but a false pride based on an exaggeration of some self generated value.

A basic step in my search for maturity was to overcome fears that were based on the apparent damages to this "False Pride" of the exaggerated values fo certain self representations.

In other words, before I could become a mature organism (individual, person, human being, man), I had to rid myself of "Hubris".

The realization that I and/or my pride were not a fragile item to be easily broken, lead me to what ever maturity I have achieved.

Although this discourse is about how and why I think as I do, there is bound to be some overlap from my propensities and those and the rest of the species?

I do not wish to change the "I" in this discourse to "WE", but as I am a part of the continuum of humanity, there is a high probability that some of my processes may be universal?

I am sure the "Hubris" is on of them.

Now back to the reasons for the title of this dichotomy, "Sexual Reproduction and Asexual/Sexual Reproduction".

The great hubris of the human male is that he is the driving force behind things, including the propagation of the race.

A great many of cultural and historical mores stem from this point of view.

I just wished to highlight that a vast majority of the species on this earth are capable of reproduction with out the male of the species.

Maybe if man (the male) could control this hubris, the species' probability of becoming extinct would lead away from zero rather that approaching it.?

I am not a feminist, or any other ist, ism, itic, or any other political or social/cultural being, or a member of any group or association that advocates ist, ism or itic, but it has come to my mind that many of the ills of man (human) and his/her endeavors have to do with various hubris' that seem to drive or motivate our activities.

I highlighted the male hubris to make the false pride point, and then laid it over the whole collective of various local organizations and the global organizations that make up our entire humanity.

Our ability to be able to cooperate in such a manner as to at least extend our chances of survival will be anchored to our ability to alleviate our visions of cultural grandeur by eliminating or at least curtailing our collective hubris.

Family/Group/Tribe/Kin and Non-Family/Group/Tribe/Kin

There seems to be an underlying propensity to differentiate how one treats family vs non-family.

This, or very similar treatment carries over to group (associations), the tribe (race?), the social divisions, the culture, subcultures and the country/nation.

There is some difference of opinion as to the basis of this altruism/kin as to its origins: genetic or cultural, or a mix of both?

For me and the purpose of this discourse on "How and Why I think as I do", the above is too general.

Interwoven in the loose tapestry of the above, are a multiple of other fibers that wolf and warp through the fabric.

A few examples: the culture/subculture conflicts e.g., various protestant religious sects, various religions in general and most curious, variations of religions in the same culture.

Something happens to the genetic propensities of kin altruism when the organism's involved splinter into diverse groups.

The question; for my purpose is, does this prove that an organism's behavior is culturally based, genetic based, or (as alluded to above), a mixture of both and if so, what ratio, and last but not least, is that ratio constant?

As it may have become apparent to you, as it has to me, that this discourse, although advocated to be an analysis of my think process, seems to be directed toward the survival or chances of survival of the species?

This is an emerging property that is/was not intentional (pre-programmed or thought out or a parallel goal of this discourse), but on too many occasions, it appears too near the core of some dichotomies not to be relevant to my thinking process?

In this light, my next question to myself is: can I prolong/aid/assure my own survival by actively thinking about my use of the dichotomy of kin/not kin, to eliminate potential obstacles in my path of survival?

This brings be to another emerging property; I seem to be overlying my net across the whole species, as if I am considering myself as a representative (average/mode/median/one among many) of the species, and as I go so goes the species.

This is/was not my goal, but as it comes up more often as I get deeper into the process of the discourse on "How and Why I think as I do", it becomes an analysis/philosophy for the species.

This is an added value, but not the reasoning behind the discourse; but, as in many things, it just is.

Statistics and Probability

In others dichotomies, I have eluded to the "magic" of emergent properties, but those are not the only "magic" in our wondrous universe; that we are able to cognize or operate on, but one of many.

This dichotomy will look into the facets of my thought processes that are connected to statistics; the phenomena's connected to the patterns of numbers and their miraculous connection to small samples, and to probability; the chance that something will happen in some relatively predictable manner or cycle.

First, statistics, a method of counting various aspects of a give range of attributes, in/on a given subject, and the relationship of a small sample of these areas, to the whole.

The most phenomenal aspect, for me anyway, of the statistical process is the bell curve.

When I operate and/or think about the functions of any system, my first concern is the capabilities and limitations of the system.

The bell curve is as perfect as this organism is capable of conceiving or organizing as representative of those capabilities and limitations, and also a graphic presentation of those aspects of the system or area under investigation that are most prevalent and/or lacking across the entire range of the items concerned.

If I am observing or studying an existing system, I can see all its strengths and/or weaknesses, and if I am planning a new system, I can design it to enhance its strengths and minimize its weaknesses from what I have learned from the statistical/graphical study of other like systems.

This brings me to the probability aspects of my universal cognitive thought process.

Given a set of fixed attributes; the various dots on the face of a die or dice, or the heads or tails on a coin, to state the simplest aspects of observing/studying probabilities of a given system and knowing, from statistically observed phenomena, I can with some assurance, predict how a given mix of objects will interact and the result of their interaction, in relationship to an intent or goal.

On of the most important (and astounding) aspects of my mind is to be able to more or less predict what another organism will do under a given set of circumstances.

There may be a built in intuitive property in the young new born organism that has a limited version of the phenomena, but it took me many years and many experiences over a broad range of individuals and situations before I reached a plateau of reading others intentions or internal emotions/feelings and what ever else is involved in their reaction to me or my presentation.

There is probably a battery of implicit operating sensual functions: visual, auditory or olfactory; that analyze the other or others, before there is explicit awareness of the situation.

The implicit functions and their reactions are (for me I am sure) based on statistical analysis and probability predictions based on all the previous exposures to the various aspects of the sensory input received from the other organism and/or other organisms.

The point of this last is that, reading another mind, both sub-consciously and consciously, is experience based, filtered through a statistical/probability function of some kind?

This carries over from simple self survival in personal one on one situation's, into broader aspects of life, socially, in business, in politics, in government, and all other facets of living.

Only by paying attention to the statistical data and the probability aspects of the data can an organism or group of organisms survive.

Again the emergent property of survival rises above my simple analysis of how and why I think as I do.

Classical Physics and Quantum Mechanics

Through out all of history, until the twentieth century, modes of measurements were based on absolutes and codified by Newtonian Physics in the 17th century.

All mathematics and scientific study was based on these "Classical Physics" parameters.

It was stated (thought) that if you knew the initial conditions of a specific event, and understood the natural laws of classical physics, you would be able to predict, absolutely, the step by step outcome of this event.

Quantum Mechanics, on the other hand, turned out to be quite different. There had to be a factored in statistical Probability and a certain uncertainty.

This uncertainty, based on the experimentally proven data, was caused by the inability of an observer to know both the position of a particle and its momentum, at the same time, along with the problem of the very observation altering the outcome, by adding or subtracting something from the system being observed.

The above, and very short and simplified descriptions of classical physics and quantum mechanics can even be reduced further for easier handling.

The universe is made up of two variations of reality (as far as I know, or as far as the premises that I operate from allow me to use),

Macro (large) reality, classical physics and Micro (small), quantum mechanics.

All the technical stuff aside, in day to day living, the macro version works very well.

On the other hand, the micro side and its ramifications make such things as weather forecasting, for example, less than perfect.

What, you ask, does this have to do with how and why I think as I do?

A good question: possibly the root to the whole reason for this discourse on self analysis of my thinking processes.

My operating premise, concerning a more or less static/discrete thought sequence, is a planning or predictive sequence returning a yes, no or maybe action, modified by other static/discrete operations that run parallel, serially and distributed through out the brain/mind, assuming Super-Consciousness rules the whole process implicitly, at the self conscious level.

This is all in the Classical Mode; given the initial/starting conditions of the particular situation, I have the ability to make and execute a workable plan.

Low and behold; however, my plans often fail, not necessarily because I don't think good, but because of the Micro influences.

I do not have all the data in a static/discrete form, from the point of view on an uncertain Micro base, plus I am not alone in this process – other organisms, systems cultures, motives, goals, etc, and other outside forces are beyond my control.

The relationship here, and the reason for including this dichotomy in the discourse, is so I don't forget the overall result of the above presentation, to my planning and ultimately, how and why I think as I do.

It is imperative for me to realize, that to function and survive, I must be very liquid and/or fluid in my outlook, and realize that the world is fuzzy (many shades of gray vs just black and white) and that this fuzziness is not necessarily a weakness on my part (that could cause panic or depression and all other kinds of hells and self doubts), but a built in, hardwired, part of the universal operating system, based on the dichotomy of Classical Physics and Quantum Mechanics, that is not always susceptible to the dialectic for an absolute synthesis.

Propensity and Destiny

Propensity and Destiny, for the purposes of this discourse, is the organism's genetic propensities and potential vs the organism's actual deterministic destiny, caused mostly by the environmental/experience mix.

Raising the organism to the Homo level, I perceive and operate on the premise that it is born with basic instincts and pre-programmed propensities to survive through evolutionary natural selection and adaptation.

All the various and overlapping functions e.g., fright/flight, kin cooperation and conflict, various species and individual related altruisms, etc., are present at birth, weighted by the chromosomal mitosis mix resulting from sexual reproduction e.g., recessive and/or dominate traits.

Given that the nature (genetic) and the nurture (embryonic) circumstances allow the organism to be birthed within the mean (average?) fitness range, the new organism will be a unique individual available for the molding that will take place thru its environmental, parental, social and cultural situation.

Within the ranges of capabilities and limitations driven by nature (the genetic side), the organism (I) will, in most be, or turn out to be what I am taught?

Using the bell curve from statistical analysis as an analogy, the organisms that fall in the mid 2/3 (67%, 33 1/3 % on either side of the mean/median) distribution, will function in the manner describe above.

The other 1/3 (the 16 2/3% at the extreme ranges of the distribution) will however be an exception to the above?

Those on the right end of the distribution will be for the most part, culturally driven fanatics, if you will, whose on the left end of the distribution will be genetic driven, and psychotic, if you will.

What the sort is, or how it is caused, is knowable, but relatively unknown, but probably will have to do with the dominate/recessive ratio of the basic "R", or pre-Homo genes?

If the primal survival functions are skewed, the result will either be psychotic (psychopath/sociopath) on one end of the spectrum, and the fanatic (ultra nationalistic, ultra patriotic, ultra religious) on the other.

The point of this dichotomy and its' relationship to the discourse is that How and Why I think as I do will fall somewhere in the middle range, for what ever hereditary and/or environmental reason, with the potential to fall to either out side range in certain circumstances, within certain contexts, in particular situations, deterministic, but not pre-destined.

Limited and Unlimited

Limited and Unlimited are relative terms when it comes to cognitive matters, but even so the concepts are very important in several areas.

I am limited in my capabilities and limitations on both ends of the spectrum – my limitations are limited by my capabilities and my capabilities are limited by my limitations, all within the range of the Homo organizational capabilities and limitations.

Notice that Unlimited is not mentioned in the above. I perceive and operate on the premise that unlimited is a misnomer in reference to physical and mental capabilities activity that have anything to do with how and why I think as I do.

I am able to operate in a deterministic manner (without pre-destiny), within the parameters and constraints of the laws of nature and certain emergent properties.

Also when I hear about "Free Will", the connotations seem absolute and therefore unlimited.

In my case, I perceive and operate on the premise (think?), that my endeavors into "Free Will" are very limited by my heredity and experience/environment.

It (my free will), is also limited by nature e.g., I can not fly without mechanical help. This is just one of many things that I can not will myself to do freely.

Wait a minute, you say, that's not what is meant by "Free Will"; "Free Will" is associated with the reactionary process and how one acts in a given situation.

I disagree; "Free Will" (the operation of) is a result of heredity propensities, capabilities and limitations, coupled with the social/cultural restraints, and the physiological and psychological state of my self at the time of the decision being made.

Free will is limited by many constraints, both internally and externally, but the overriding factor here, from my point of view of how and why I think as I do, is not necessarily the value or limitations of "Free Will", but the overriding fact that I am always responsible for my own acts, what ever the range of my "Free Will" was/is involved.

My point here is that I do not have the "Free Will" to commit a vile act, of what ever kind, without bearing the responsibility.

The Idea that evil exists because of "Free Will" just doesn't work.

Evil is a matter of the lack of responsibility on the one/ones perpetrating it, within the range of one/ones limitations.

One may have no choice?

Finite and Infinite

Finite and Infinite, words/concepts that I hear and use often; but, just what are their ramifications; really, when they are used together and/or separately?

When I say finite, do I mean known, limited, precise and fixed, and do I mean by infinite, unknown, unlimited, fuzzy and variable, or am I only referring to the limits of whole numbers?

Or, on the other hand, am I referring to the data I am able to internalize and use vs the totality of the universal data?

A point I am trying to make here, is that in my thinking process, context and/or situational orientation may be (is?) as or more important than concepts and/or specific meanings.

The focus, at the moment, a discrete/static point of departure made up of previously sorted and condensed data is the driving force of concepts/ meanings, usage, (more about this in another dichotomy).

As with many things/objects/concepts, it is different strokes for different folks, in the sense that within me, there are a myriad of "SELF'S" neither finite or infinite, driven by different forces.

Internal and External

Perhaps the most basic and important dichotomy of all, Internal and External are the very basis of life.

The single cell organism cannot exist without closure between itself and the outside world.

This closure is circumstanced by a malleable membrane that separates the internal from the external.

The membrane allows resources in and toxin out.

As an aside, without the ability to exclude/extrude toxins, no organism can survive. This capability may be one of the basics of the emergence of life.

The Internal and External dichotomy is not limited to the single celled organism, but is present at every link of the chain from single cell to the multicellular organisms, to individuals (I), families, tribes, societies, cities, states, countries and all the subunits that make up the those various entities e.g., religions, political parties, union and other associations, marriages, governments, business corporation, etc.

From the point of view of this discourse, this dichotomy covers the basic ranges between self interest and the interests of the various and sundry components (External and Internal), that help to perpetuate survival.

A point walked around and poked at throughout this discourse, but not stated - a question - why do I think like I do — the answer: to survive.

So what it is down to now is not why I think as I do, but how do I think as I do?

Although they are so intertwined, I will try to stress the how do I think facets as much as possible, to get at the heart of Self, and why Self, and how Self (an internal?), is connected to the thinking process, a super conscious administration of the various sub conscious states.

This will be, and is, what this entire self analyzing discourse is about, and all that has come before and all that comes after are dedicated to the above statement.

Stability and Instability

Being stable or unstable are two more concepts that can cover a broad range of representations, and are synonymous (analogy wise) with many other dichotomies.

In analyzing my thinking process, I am finding more and more simple dichotomies not to be simple after all.

It's beginning to dawn on me that this attribute of language/ semantic variability of meaning and usage may be the basis of humanness.

Rather than the more simple responses to these meanings/usages; then, do/did, in the realm of "R", organisms with a complex pre-frontal cortex (Homo?), evolve the ability to weigh and shade concept/meaning, through language, both internal and external, to use basic stereotype representations to weave complex and differentiated planning scenarios from a relatively few basic building blocks?

A merging of the built in, hardwired "R" functions magnified, from the unconscious to the super conscious, into the elaborate processes that make possible this thing I call "SELF"?

I know I have digressed from stability and instability; but, while writing these dichotomies my train of thought some times wanders to the bigger picture of all the dichotomies and their function as part of my thinking process, and I write them down so I won't loose them.

The reader(s), (if you/they are still with me) will have to refer (mentally) back to the prologue, where I stated that while the dichotomies were intended to stand alone, there was/is/will be overlap, digression, duplication and contradiction.

Because concept/meaning driven actions are contextually based; and, while things are alike, they are not always the same, at least from my perspective and operating premises.

Back to Stability and Instability:

In the simplest sense, stability is predictable and instability is not, but in most cases there is more than either/or.

This is so circular, that I must stop!

The point I am trying to make here to you and myself (as I may have alluded to, or you may have surmised, through out this entire discourse, I am talking to you and myself), is to keep it simple without disallowing the potential variability of a given situation based on the concept/content contest.

WOW!!

Continuous and Discrete

Continuous and Discrete are very important concepts, each in their own right and also as the components of a system whole.

Continuous can (from my perspective) be viewed as a flowing, fluid phenomena, such as a river, or time, or even life.

Discrete, on the other hand, seems to have the attitude of stasis; that is, it is a situation frozen in time on the one hand, while being self involved and perhaps secretive, depending on the semantics involved.

The value of this dichotomy, in my analysis of how and why I think as I do, is that while the thinking process seems continuous, it is really not. It proceeds (very rapidly, so as to seem continuous) throughout the body/brain/mind systems in discrete/static steps within and without various parallel, serial, and distributed systems.

Various sensual inputs, combined with chemical, electrical, hormonal, nervous system, memory, recall of previously experienced discrete activities; join, merge, enhance and suppress each other in the various layers/levels of the subconscious before they percolate up into the super conscious and I become aware of a thought.

In another dichotomy, I will look at Quantum Discrete and Continuous, but for now I am presenting this on/in the classical physics sense i.e., if you are aware on the initial/starting conditions of a system, you can predict the outcome.

I am operating on the premise that the built in hardware and evolutionary driven discrete generic situations of the organism's (I) operating systems in my body/brain/mind, operate, within deterministic (but not predestined) parameters, on the data bases (cultural and environmentally driven, if you will) acquired through life experiences.

At any given (discrete) moment, the operating system/hardware/ data base function is influenced by external sensory input.

From our finite perspective, this process is instantaneous, but in reality is is not.

Although alluding to the body as being machine like, and/or computer like, are just analogies, there is a very precise (within parameters) step by step operation going on.

This is important to my thinking process, because at every discrete/ static moment in the seemingly continuous flow, the various aspects of the body/brain/mind e.g., new external input, and old stored and recalled data, emotions/feelings, hormones/adrenalin, etc, are influencing the next step in the process.

As stated before, a vast majority of these activities are subconscious and not available to my "Self".

My thinking process, my "Free Will" (if you will), is not driven by my super conscious alone, but is edited and limited by those subconscious, built in hardware/operating systems and their data bases.

In a word, once again, how and why I think as I do is an 80/20 proposition, 80% of the process is out of my hands at any given moment, but can be managed by the other 20%, if I pay attention and focus, not only locally, but also globally, for the short term and the long term aspects of my decision and/or plan, goals.

As an aside, again, these dichotomies are not just the definitions of the terms involved, but seem to morph into a system with a life of its own, and have emergent properties that weren't intended in the initial concept for this method of presenting my discourse.

Particle Location
and Particle Velocity

Particle Location and Particle Velocity are associated with sub atomic particles and the ability of knowing where a particle is located and/or how fast it is moving, (velocity/momentum).

Investigation has shown that the methods available for the observation of those phenomena, won't/don't allow both phenomena to be observed at the same time i.e., If you know where a particle is, you don't know how fast it is moving, and on the other hand, you know how fast it is moving (usually 'c', the speed of light (photons)), you don't/can't know its precise position.

This quandary is called the "Heisenberg uncertainty principle".

Again, you ask, what has this to do with how and why do I think as I do?

The scientific method, through understanding the uncertainty principle, is not able to make precise predictions: The functions of the scientific method and also the functions of the thought process; have harnessed the "magic" of the statistical/probability properties, that seem to be part of the laws of nature, to base their predictions.

Given the probability that a data set is accurate and operates within a given range, it is accepted for predictions. This has been experimentally proven and has assumed axiomatic status.

This function is analogous to fuzzy logic, which is analogous to the weighted neural network process of the brain that gives rise to the subconscious modules/modality of the body/brain/mind, which in turn gives rise to the super conscious, the level that "self" (I), operate.

The point of all this circular rhetoric is that the decisions I make (steps to reach a goal), are based on the probability that the data involved is both correct (position) and has been timely and interpreted properly (speed/momentum) in order to allow my predictions/plans/concepts of reality to be valid, and ultimately increase or at least maintain the level of fitness necessary for my survival.

Again, the same point is reached, the bottom line reason of how and why I think as I do, is to survive and have reproductive success, probably not through or from a personal volition, but from the evolutional history of natural selection/adaptation merged with cultural evolution.

Description and Explanation

Description and Explanation are the epitome of dichotomies.

To describe something is usually a spatial/temporal or textural definition of the object in question.

Where is it, what does it look like, is it alive or dead (organic or inorganic), have an odor or make a noise?

On the other hand explanation has to do with the function of the object or organism.

What is it for, what does it do, can I use it for my benefit or can it be detrimental to me?

These terms (description and explanation) are often mixed, merged, or interchanged for one another.

In the thinking process, I find that if I confuse the usages, a decision or plan can go one way or another, depending on the basis I use to define/analyze the object or organism.

This is just the tip of the iceberg on not having semantic closure i.e., the phenomena of different groups (or disciplines) using the same word or words to define/analyze very different subjects, concept and/or systems.

In a word, they don't speak the same language.

Now back to my thinking process:

As my thinking process depends very much on the external data presented to me by various media, that may or may not have semantic closure, my data base may be or has been contaminated by contrary, contradictory, mutually exclusive data points, that can, have, or will cause my plans, predictions and/or conclusions to be false or at least faulty.

This would/could be very troublesome to me if it weren't for the multiple representations that are available to the subconscious.

They (the subconscious processes that mediate my implicit self) can weigh the differences and sometimes (most of the time), since I have become a mature adult, eliminate many of the new external representation that do no agree, and modify the rest or at least inhibit them awaiting further evidence of their validity or at least their correspondence to other stored representations that have shown evidence of adding to the robustness of the systems that aid and abet survival.

This is good; however, the lack of semantic closure can still cause confusion and ambiguity in my thinking process.

If I am able to overcome these fallacies, this is where innovation, creativity and/or added value ideas or new representations come from.

Name (word) and Concept

I have always heard that if you didn't have the word, you couldn't have the concept.

I find that it is more like; if I can't recall the word, I can't get a good grip on the concept.

On the other hand, I find myself recalling a/the concept, but cannot recall the word to describe it.

This phenomenon leads me to the premise that my cognitive processes are hierarchically driven i.e., deductive, from the general (the word) to the particular (the concept).

In computereze, a do loop, if, then, do; if you have the name, then do the concept.

However, as stated above, I sometimes have the concept (dimly?), but can't put a name on it for communications purposes, either internally or externally (implicitly or explicitly).

This feedback loop (more computerize) process has to be a very vital aspect of survival i.e., if you can't get to the data through the name, in order not to hesitate and put my organism in jeopardy, garner the fuzzy data (dimly perceived concept) and grasp the name later.

This parallel/serial/distributed processing is likely the emergent property(s) that helps raise the various subconscious (implicit) processes to the super conscious (explicit) state(s) that allow "self" representation.

This is one of the main reasons to strive for semantic closure across multiple fields (disciplines) of endeavors, scientific, social and cultural, in order to insure that the collective "self" along with the individual "self" is, so to speak, on the same page.

This came ever more clearly to me while I was researching the literature on cognition, consciousness, intelligence, the mind, neural science, etc.

While I have described, by definition, for my purposes, from my premises, that I am first awake/conscious, then function implicitly in the sub conscious through 80% of the operating process (using the 80/20 heuristic rule of thumb) and explicitly the other 20% in the super conscious.

The above mentioned literature, break these three levels into many more, which is fine for defining discrete/static detail and connectedness, but the problem is the names of these levels and/ or the number of these levels is vastly different from discipline to discipline.

Outside investigators (I) are/am not always able to assign like concepts to like concepts because of these naming procedures that are not semantically closed.

From My perspective, this seems extremely inefficient and tells me that the individuals working within the various disciplines (local) are really not maximizing their efforts (global) due to this lack of consensus (semantic closure).

In the past, when much research was done in isolation and communications were slow, there was reason for this, but with the computer age, and the internet and the World Wide Web this phenomena should have long ceased.

It hasn't; which, from my point of view, reviewing my internal processes concerning the difference between rationalization and reasoning i.e., to rationalize, one is goal oriented and only uses the data points that lead to the preconceived goal, while reasoning allows/demands the use of all the available data points and follows them to what ever end conclusion.

The former (rationalization) is done internally, by using ones own names and concepts, while the latter (reasoning), being external, uses universal names and concepts.

If there is no universal names and concepts (semantic closure across disciplines) then there can be no reasonable outcome?

Please note that the above was written with the understanding that each individual or group, due to various prestige and economic pressures, must keep their research confidential, that even when it is in the public domain, there is still too little being done to insure semantic closure across disciplines.

Symmetry and Asymmetry

Symmetry and Asymmetry are basically the right or left handedness (mirror image) of things or those that only appear in nature as either left handed or right handed.

These concepts are very powerful in the higher scientific endeavors, but that is not their only use for my purposes, in this discourse.

Symmetric and Sync are analogous, and this is the usage (semantic closure?) that I put them to use in the analyzing my thinking process.

In order to come to a "good" decision or to plan properly, or to prophesize the future activities of a fellow organism, I have be in sync, or balanced in the evaluation of the implicit (subconscious) inputs vs the (super conscious) explicit inputs that must be played off against recalled representation of like situation and/or scenarios.

They have to be in sync (symmetric), if they are to be useful implicitly, but on the other hand, if they are asymmetric, then the explicit (super conscious) must override the implicit (sub conscious) inclinations i.e., if a set of like data points are asymmetric, action potentials can/must be changed and a new set of representations will/can be stored for later recall to help fine tune the decision, planning or prophesizing process.

I am not sure what the balance is between implicit and explicit "self", but I do know that there are times when minor doubt or confusion or hesitation take place in seemingly simple and standard operation procedures (more computereze) I have/get fuzzy/ambivalent feelings.

I am not sure if biological evolution or cultural evolution or both (probably) are the basis for this phenomenon, but I perceive and operate on the premise (think) that it is a function of symmetric and/or asymmetric quantum level, sub atomic particles operating on a probability basis that allows for this fine tuning to arise.

This is not a level of the sub conscious that has been investigated or mentioned in the literature I have read, but given that a good part of these processes are driven by chemical/electrical impulses, the ion make up of the chemical compounds may/must have something to do with the weight of an action potential?

I feel very strongly i.e., I perceive the above and my operating premise in this area is very positively weighted, that the "Laws of Nature" are such that emerging properties; the super conscious for one, are mitigated and/or associated with the activities of the basic sub atomic particles that are ubiquitous within the universe, and they should not be forgotten or overlooked in the higher levels of my own thought process.

Sensor or Censor

Sensor and Censor are not really dichotomies, but they are much related to the subject of many dichotomies i.e., Semantic Closure.

Normally, these terms as spoken, sound the same, (to me?) sensor and sensor?

It is only in context or when written that their meanings are clear.

I bring this up in relationship to personal/interpersonal communication vs reading the written word.

In word association without context, the spoken Sensor/Censor word can give a false representation via the normal external to internal flow.

If they are part of a list, arbitrarily chosen, implying one or the other concepts (words/names/labels) Sensor/Censor, the weight of those several words (in my case) leads me to assume, if the several words involved have to do with seeing, the "sensor/censor" word I hear from the verbal list will be interpreted as "Sensor".

My point; here, is that language (at least English) through a wonderfully broad and deep body of communications capabilities, has the weakness of need of context and semantic closure to make a statement clear and precise, from the speaker to the hearer.

What I perceive e.g., have heard, read, or seen on/in visual media – TV, Movies, etc, is not necessarily what the sending medium, person or visual story had in mind.

Because there are many copies of many different representations stored in long term memory, much of the time I am able to cognize the appropriate and matching Super Conscious reaction to the input.

However; and this is really important, from the point of view of How and Why I Think as I do, some heavily weighted representations; more than is good for stable "truth" of understanding, were formed when my personal data base was very small: think; "If I have a child until he/she is five years old I will shape their ethics code and moral responses and sense of right or wrong perspectives, and those heavily weighted early representations; also new, unrelated to previous data, bad inputs or interpretations, cause me to have a built in (in computereze, hardwired) parochial bias and or prejudice in the area and/or coverage of these false, bad, weak, or inappropriate representations.

Again; the point, I am what I perceive. First, at the various unconscious (Sub Conscious) hierarchal levels (that ~80% of value assessment) and second at the Super Conscious level (that ~20% of the value assessment), even in the presence of fresh relevant data, in many cases the ~80% will still override the ~20% of representational value and I may never be able to override the parochial bias and/or prejudice of the heavy weight erroneous or faulty representations.

In some cases, what I am trying to say, you can't change my mind.

If the person(s) I am dealing with don't have some understanding of the above, associations and friendships can be harmed or terminated.

Therefore; I caution myself, when I deal with others who are adamant about a subject where I know they are dead wrong, I try to exercise tolerance and avoid these subjects, or at least take them with a grain of salt, if I value the association or relationship.

I am very ambivalent about this personal hypocrisy, but have to live with it to maximize my very survival?

Pain and Pleasure

Pain and Pleasure, on the surface, seem to be a simple dichotomy, the first hurts and the second makes me feel good or at least better.

But this is an internal action/activity within a single organism, with reflection on the external continence i.e., if I feel good I smile.

But; again, it's not that simple, pain can be physical and/or mental and mediated from within, about ones self, or initiated from an external source, while pleasure, though sometimes self generated (by reflection on some stored/recalled representation), is mostly, in my case, fed from external sources e.g., beauty in its various manifestations: music, art, a flower, a pretty face or a comely body, the summer sky or the nights mysterious glitter and glimmer.

And, a third facet of the pain/pleasure phenomena is the pleasure I feel from someone else's pain, if I feel that they deserve it.

The real essence of the pain/pleasure dichotomy is my physiological responses to the source(s) of the pain/pleasure that are both physical manifestations and/or   mental constraints (Constructs).

The Pain and Pleasure dichotomy brings out the fact that physical manifestations and mental constructs are a/the driving force(s) behind the fitness to survive i.e., why do, or why am I motivated to survive?

Is it the pleasure I get from living, or the fear of the pain of dying?

Or, is it a mix of both, in that the sometimes painful labors necessary for survival give way to the pleasures of survival?

Are pain and pleasure a dichotomy at all, or are they the synthesis of some dialectic process of emergent properties that drive (motivate) me to continue living (to survive)?

Again, as I get into the analysis of the various dichotomies, I find myself ending more and more of them with the survival theme.

I ask myself, am I an organism that is driven by the very "Law of Nature", to survive or is it an emergent property that those who commit suicide, loose or lack?

I know that I am one among many, and am also unique in my own manner, but is there connectivity within the broad brush stroke of life that makes my reflections complementary with all life, or at least with the Homo species, and is the Pain and Pleasure dichotomy the fabric of that connectivity?

There must be more here than I have found, maybe later dichotomies or recollections/reflections will help me find it?

Analytic and Synthetic

Analyze and synthesize are the first synonyms that come to my mind when thinking of the Analytic and Synthetic dichotomy.

On another hand, analytic is the method of going from the general to the specific e.g., logical deduction, while synthetic, in the modern vernacular is pseudo, or fake, or alike, or a substitute, because of feel or appearance, such as nylon i.e., synthetic silk.

There is also a correlation between gathering (analyzing) and the synthesis of a compound, (putting together all its parts).

This dichotomy is another look at the language and semantic closure, in that the "common" usages of words are not necessarily the representation of my internal milieu.

If I am not carefully following the context of a conversation, lecture, explanation, or the written word, I may attach a different weight to the words (terms/concepts) analytic and/or synthesis.

On the one hand, the ability of my mind, during the thought process, to handle this sort of thing is the norm; however, in cross discipline semantic situations, it can cause confusion and misunderstanding and lead to rhetorical conflicts and ill will, to the extreme.

My reason for concern about this subject; although, not the basic reason for doing this dichotomy, is that it is possible for me to misunderstand the/a concept(s) due to semantic break down. Can I trust myself to make the right decision, or set the right goal(s), or plan properly, or predict another organism's future response, or even exercise "Free Will" if I am operating on a wrong premise due to fuzzy semantics?

In my case, as I have stated before, I believe or disbelieve nothing, because I am finite and the universal data base is, from my perspective, infinite, and therefore I can never have enough data to know or discern the "Truth", so I must operate from my own mental construct, that I call "operating on the premise that…". If my mental construct is based on faulty representations of the current external input vs implicit internal recall, the result will be a faulty decision.

The important result of this/these dichotomic analysis is that during the writing process I fall into the/a philosophical mode, where my thinking slows down and becomes clearer and I am able to "reset" (more computereze), some faulty representations, at least on paper.

I perceive this as an emergent property of my thinking process and is basic to "How and Why I Think as I do".

Listability and Compatibility

Listability and Compatibility have to do with the ability to compromise.

In the Dialectic, I start with a thesis (Listability) and antitheses (Listability) and (optimally) end up with synthesis (Compatibility).

If the thesis and/or antitheses have lists that contain mutually exclusive ideas, is the outcome synthesis or deadlock?

I have seen nowhere, involving the Dialectic, any reference to this issue; although, this doesn't mean there are none?

I have set a premise, that given that diplomacy is the highest/finest of the Dialectic arts, war is the meeting of the mutual exclusives of the Listability Function of the original dialogue.

This thought; however, is only valid given a dialogue between rational organisms or societies with compatible cultures.

The diplomatic version of the dialectic may not work in a situation without a function of might is right?

Within the ranges of the above, in reference to, "How and Why I Thinks as I do", and the conclusion that I have come to, that it is driven by the need to survive, I must also assume that if I am in a subordinate position I must put my mutually exclusive aside (or at least on hold) to achieve synthesis.

This is a surface thought and conclusion, while deeper thinking brings to mind, that in my case, as what I "Think" or "Believe" are but operating premise, mental constructs, if you will, with no connection to emotion or proprietary conviction.

My premise's are so liquid and/or fluid that any circumstances or situational context that lessons my fitness (from my prospective), for survival will allow me to operate in/on what ever premise that would/will maximize my fitness for survival, without my losing any self esteem or entering into any psychological trauma that would decrease my fitness for survival.

This may be, or seem to be circular at best, and not even relevant to the original dichotomy at worst, but none the less, how I think, and once again, the why, is based on the survival of my organism!

Why Not Both and/or
It Can't Be Both

In many previous dichotomies I have alluded to the dialectic.

In this dichotomy concerning "why not both and/or it can't be both", I will try to look again at the basic ideas involved with the dialectic and dichotomies.

In the dichotomy on "Listability and Compatibility", I observed, that in my case, mutually exclusive item on my list are eliminated (or at least overlooked for now) in the light of survival.

In this dichotomy I wish to look further in this issue.

I have often heard, "well, you can't have it both ways", on the other hand I have asked the question, "why not both"?

Within the realm of "How and Why I Think as I Do", there is the aspect of getting along with others.

Do I want to go along, to get along, and how does this relate to the individuals in the society, and/or cultural/multicultural arenas?

I have come to the conclusion that although it cannot always be both ways, because in the multi-cultural realm there is so much variance in mutually exclusive lists, that if there is going to be any meaningful interaction, one culture, political entity, individual, society or what ever, must allow some leeway (some of both?) or neither will survive.

This, in many cases, is a factor of economics (available and usable resources), even at the level of the single organism, my self.

I am not above operating on the premise, or at least a very basic, high potential premise that, "it's all economic".

Once again, over and over again, an organisms (groups of organism, on average?), most of the time will opt for the solution that enhances their fitness for survival.

An example of this is the ability (operational fact) for liberal democratic states to do business with totalitarian and/or authoritarian regimes with necessary resources, for the survival of both.

Another, short term look, in the diplomatic realm, of individual (or states?), the enemy of my enemy is my (current?) friend.

I don't necessarily hold with the above statement as a core premise, but survival (in the short term), is often covered by gray, fuzzy, overlapping, conflicting, contradictory, nebulous (temporary?), premise(s).

Unknown Cause and Effect

I deal with Cause and Effect in another dichotomy, but known Cause and Effect are not the same as Unknown Cause and Effect.

While dealing with "How and Why I Think as I do", I have touched on the ubiquitous 80/20 hubristic of sub/unconscious implicit operations that go on in the brain/mind (sometimes labeled as "The Old Brain" or "R") before they get to the Neo-Cortex and become explicit (the Super-Conscious function/emergent property?).

The effect (implicit) representations are, as far as I am normally concerned without deep meditation and/or before bio-feedback operations, derived from "Unknown Cause".

I perceive, and operate on the premises that there are several layers of Knowledge e.g., The Unknowable, The Knowable, but Unknown, and the Known.

When I allude to "Unknown" (in this case?), I am operating in the past/present mode, but not future mode.

When explicate representations rise to the Super Conscious, I am operating in the now (present), from past (sub/unconscious) data, but when I stop and analyze these present representations, I can often bring to the explicit level, some of the previously implicit (sub/conscious) causes (unknown causes) and they then become (present/future?) more or less known.

The point (question?) here is not only for the purposes of this discourse; but, can I discern, in general, "How and Why I Think as I do". In the incidence above am I sometimes able to get at the details behind the explicate (Super-Conscious, pre-frontal driven?) explicated representations?

This process moves the basically implicit, sub/unconscious representations, the ones that have become explicitly available, into a "working memory" data base(s), that are presently (forever?) available for any future analysis that I make, or wish to make.

What I am trying to say, is that through self analysis, I am able to move some of the unknown causes of my thinking process to the realm of the known.

Is to know myself: to stop and contemplate what is behind a current and present representation; and ascertain, is it logical and "The Truth" in accordance with my overall perception of who I am or want to be, or should I look even deeper, to determine the unknown cause that is allowing me to deviate from the perceived "Norm" that I wish to maintain, and modify it through (by) bringing it into permanent working memory, so it won't continue to warp my thinking process in the future?

My main (and very important) point here is, I have (have I?) discovered a way to modify my parochial biases & prejudices, to bring them more in line with general reality and also (perhaps) the changing and modified social/cultural trends.

Left Brain vs Right Brain

There has been much said about the Right Brain/Left Brain traits/activities; separations of power, if you will.

I have wondered how the Right Brain/Left Brain dichotomy effects "How and Why I think as I do"?

If the left brain handles speech and language skills (capabilities and limitations), my left brain is the dominate factor in my thinking. Although I only speak/read English, I have a pretty good handle on some foreign words and phrases.

On the other hand, or brain hemisphere, as it were, it is said that the right brain controls or at least mediates the spacial representations.

I cannot picture, mentally, objects that I understand from the literature, many others can?

I assume that they can hold these objects for a sustained duration, while I only get a fuzzy, minute glance at best.

I have also heard/read that drawing, music and mathematics are right brain functions.

It may be said that the Left Brain is digital and discrete, and that the Right Brain is Analog and continuous?

From my point of view, appreciations of the above items are left brain, even if their creation is a right brain function.

Given the last statement, I operate on/under/from the premise that even though the right brain controls the left side of the body (symmetry), and left eye (also symmetry), and the left brain controls the right, I feel, at least in my case, that "How and Why I Think as I do" is a balance between the two hemispheres that cannot generally be separated, although, there may be a weighted propensity of one or the other to influence a certain process; the overall, final results formulated in the explicit representations of the neo (prefrontal) cortex (that I perceive to be a single entity), overlaps both hemispheres.

As I have noted in other dichotomies, I do not advocate there is any value to my   theories, or if they are factual and/or truthful, just that they are the premises that I operate from.

Biological Reproduction vs Biological Economics

Biological Reproduction vs Biological Economics may not seem relevant to "How and Why I Think as I do", but I have only alluded, so far, in this discourse, to my personal survival (Biological Economics), while the other side of the coin is progeny survival, that cannot happen without (in my case) Biological Reproduction.

The main connection between Biological Reproduction and Biological Economics is; can I afford to reproduce, and how much?

This may seem pretty straight forward at first glance, but this macro view can be deceiving.

On the micro level; the level of the details and harsh reality of the survival of the fittest, and their adaptation niche, brings out the beginnings of what I call my moral/ethical groundings.

Metaphorically and allegorically, for me or my progeny to survive, something else must die, be it plant or animal, plus, given various situations with the current environment and the number of progeny, how many organisms can the environment/ecology support?

Do I have to sacrifice some progeny in order for the rest to live, or all of them, so I can live to reproduce again in the future, or will I sacrifice the long term ecology for the short term reproduction cycle?

I perceive and operate on the premise that early in the evolution process this activity was built on or chosen (natural selection) in those organisms that acted (through instinct or random trial and error, or both, in what ever order), in the fittest manner to insure a balance of reproductive success and ecological stability and that this activity did become instinctive up to the "R" phase of evolution (given that my operating premise excepts that an increase in organismal complexity is classified as an upward direction), and remained un/subconscious and/or implicit, until at some point the concept became operational explicitly in the Super Conscious.

These activities became not only moral/ethical groundings in nature, but the vary basis of conscience itself.

The bottom line, again becoming a mix of my basic human nature, modified by environmental experience, directed toward my survival and reproductive success.

As an aside, in a later part of this discourse, I will present some vignettes on "What I Think", based on what I discover about "How and Why I Think as I do", and touch on the possible reasons for my, and of course, other organisms needs to survive.

Quantum Continuous vs Quantum Discreteness or Stasis

As macro and micro systems/worlds/concepts differ in size/scale and various other attributes, also does Quantum Continuous and Quantum discreteness or stasis.

In the quantum realm there are very short discrete/static periods within and almost continuous uncertain statistical/probable situations.

Non the less, at a small enough and slow enough level, the quantum phenomena within the individual (and collective??) atom(s) there is/are very precise and controlled steps (following the natural laws) operating very much like my free will, in that, for some duration, what has happened in the near past determines (within non predestined parameters) at the local level, perhaps driven (within only natural law allowable parameters) from the global situation.

My point, I think (?), is that is that although there is an uncertain outcome and variation at the micro level that carries over to the macro level and allows an overall determinate, but not predestined outcome, the natural laws driving particle (sub-atomic) activities are based on discrete/static step by step operations, perhaps constrained by the compound and/or molecules involved.

The bottom line is; from my perspective and from the premises I operate on, that the creative force(s) that initiated my (our) situation (universe(s)), initiated a set of conditions: (more redundancy) the initial conditions that were too and are operating within a deterministic, but not predetermined ranges.

Once again, using the analogy free will, I am able to operate freely within the range of environmental constraints, coupled with generic propensity, dampened and/or enhanced by experience, cultural and various contextual circumstances.

I have a lot of latitude, but it is probably based on the first five and/or pre-teen years of my parental/environmental/ cultural/ experience. Perhaps the grounding of my parochial biases and basic prejudges.

And last but not least, there are structural components involved e.g., I cannot fly on my own!

Label/Name/Symbol
and Objective Functionality

In order to differentiate representations explicitly, I find that I assign implicit representations with a name for identity, a symbol for recognition and a label for conceptualization.

The transfer from the nebulas implicit into the explicit adds an objective weight or functionality to their values and/or meanings i.e., implicitly these representations are subjective, as they are make up of the results of many action potentials, modified and/or codified and pushed from the un/subconscious to Super Consciousness explicit and objective and functional representations that I operate on/with.

This transference happens in a transient place (an emerging property?) between the un/subconscious and the Super Conscious, that I call the Spacial Conscious (a concept that may be unique to me (or not)), perhaps via the Broca/Wernicke areas that give rise to the verbal translation between the implicit and the explicit?

I have called this facet of consciousness Spacial, because the phenomena (for me)is of a short duration, in an unknown location akin to my spacial capabilities i.e., when I try to visualize (get) a mental picture of, say a number (symbol), it is very thin, rapid and gone. I am unable to hold the mental representation, where as if I am recalling a previously seen number, such as an address, I can hold it longer.

What I am trying to say here, and not very will so far, is that there are ranges of differences between direct recall of a complete incident vs the initiation of a new incidence based on the various pieces or recollected pixels and bits (again in computereze) from other and perhaps not associated or directly attached to the final explicit product, but at the point of expicitcy, they acquire a name, symbol and label and an objective functionality into the now of the self response.

Once again, I did not do this well, but I hope that the same function/process that novelists use to give half the story line and let the reader fill in the rest is able to work here.

It will not work if I am absolutely unique, but if I am one of many, with overlapping attributes, a mean or average function may allow the reader to follow my thought process, if not, not!

The Robin (Dinosaur) and The Chipmunk (Mammal)

This dichotomy will wander even further afield than some of the others, but I still feel that it is valid as to "How and Why I Think as I do", at least in part.

The Robin is one of the evolutionary results of decent from the Dinosaurs, actions that encompass a period of growth changes from small reptiles to the vastly large dinosaurs and back again to the relatively small robin.

The chipmunk, on the other hand (from my perspective and operating premise) is very closely related to the mammals that co-existed with the dinosaurs.

There is also another facet (or facets), to this evolutionary flow. Both these lines had a unique common ancestor that at some point gave rise to the branching that allowed the mammal branch to retain the "R" (reptilian low or old brain) feature(s).

I think (operate on the premise) that it is important that I know and realize that the (or a) basis of my thinking process is closely related to other complex multicellular organisms, and is based on survival.

This is not the first time I have referred to survival as a driving force behind the why of my thinking process.

I emphasize this over and over again, to reinforce the weighted forces between heredity and environment, nature and nurture, genetic propensity and cultural adaptation.

I am not a blank slate (tabula rasa or sacred tablet), written on and/or conditioned by my environment and/or culture, but an organism with built in functionality that allows me to modify the external input and/or data to such a point that they do not override my need to survive.

As an aside, I also realize that some organisms in other cultures and/or circumstances are able to sacrifice for the greater good of the group, family, tribe, etc., such as military personal, parents who give away, sell or kill or let die some of their offspring so the rest can survive, or in the case of the suicide bombers who sacrifice (martyr) themselves for the greater good and a reward in the after life.

This not withstanding, they are not me, and as this discourse is on "How and Why I Think as I do", I feel, I perceive, and I operate on the premise that though I am unique, I am still one among many, who most of the time, under most circumstances are motivated by self survival.

Assimilation and Differentiation

A really serious dichotomy: the need to belong; the social instinct, but also the need to be an individual, as in post adolescence, but a member in good standing in ones peer group.

My operating premise is that the EGO is a/the much faceted driving force involved in these phenomena.

Look at me, me, me, as a unique individual, but also look at me, I belong, or look at me, the top dog, or on the down side, no good things ever happen to me, my group or my ideas.

I operate on the premise that the ambiguity, this balance, if you will, between self and group is a manifestation of the individual organisms need to reproduce, while on the other hand the genetic (seemingly) propensity for kin affection.

Once again, it boils down to survival: what direction, assimilation or differentiation will enhance my success and/or survival or my progeny survival, while at the same time fulfill my need for personal pleasure/satisfaction, a sometimes overriding driving force?

Intrinsic and Extrinsic

As implicit and explicit are related to un/subconscious and super conscious facets of the thought process, intrinsic and extrinsic are the two sides of impulse functions.

I perceive that as the Neo Cortex evolved into anterior and posterior sections, the Pre-Frontal Cortex started to house the functions of the explicit self, while "R" remained in charge of the basic, at the moment implicit activities, the posterior Neo-Cortex started to house extrinsic scenario's of implicitly, a memory bank, if you will, of the chains of intrinsic (instinctive) motivations that had worked in the past, an array (back to computerize) or table of group actions rather than single impulses that enhance survival.

Those organisms that mutated to or inherited the variations of these functions survived more often than not.

Perhaps the posterior Neo Cortex came first, and by working so well gave rise, through further mutation and structural availability, to the anterior Neo Cortex (Pre-Frontal) and was the initial force behind Super Consciousness?

I have seen no scientific studies that indicate the above, but non-the-less these are the premises that I operate from, and their influence should be seen throughout this discourse.

All that has gone before and any after, are innovation and or extrapolations of what I have read, or my interpretation and understanding of that reading.

Individual Reason
and Universal Reason

Individual Reason(ing) and Universal Reason(ing), for my purposes, in this discourse, are the dichotomy between the way I think and that relationship with the thoughts about the same matters, as the rest of humanity.

Perhaps I should say the vast majority of the rest of humanity, because there is sure to be a small majority, for what ever psychological reason, who don't think like the vast majority.

My take on this is the 10% (?), who don't get the word. That may even be getting larger; if some of the more fanatic (and perhaps growing) lunatic fringe is any indication.

As an aside, I am also aware this minority may be a new trend in the Human Nature/Cultural mix and may be becoming the new universal majority?

If this is the case, I am operating on the premise that the species (Homo) will go the way of the more than 99.9% (a scientific estimate?) of all the other extinct species that have once thrived of earth.

This, not withstanding, is a digression from the point that I am exploring.

Is there a normal range of universal thinking across individuals, societies and cultures?

I am aware and understand that the cultures of the world are vastly different; but, are these differences absolute, or are they a façade, under laid by a universal survival method of instructions and cognitions that are alike, while the cultural surface adaptations are just variations of those methods of the survival apparatus?

The question is, can a global society be maintained by the very existence of a universal thought process that can be utilized by the dialectic (again my favorite mental tool) to achieve a world synthesis that will allow the species to prosper and remain extant?

The bottom line, and once again, the purpose of this entire discourse: is How and Why I think the way I do compatible with the rest of my society/culture and carried over to other cultures?

For me this is an important question and (besides the ego trip of having a book in print), a main reason for this discourse in the first place, along side of my finding out about myself through the writing, is how do you, the reader feel about the work?

If you don' like it or can't utilize any of what I have done here, and don't buy (or buy), my discourse, I will know that it doesn't matter How and Why I think, because I am a fringe variation and will not survive to carry my thinking process on to other generations.

What do I think about?

At the end of the preface I mentioned that while the inception and motivation behind this discourse was to find out "How and Why I think as I Do", the process gave rise to the emerging property of what I think about certain facets of the human condition?

The following vignettes will cover what I perceive as important to me, (it's all about me), I am sure that you, the reader, have discovered this already. This is a Self centered dialogue with my self, about my self; with some reference to the possible overlap between me and the rest of the species.

About Theology –
Then my Premise – Then Religion

Using the first line of The Book of Genesis as a starting point i.e., "In the beginning", theology is a look at the conditions before the "Beginning".

Being finite, I had a beginning, am having duration and will have an end in my present form.

Being finite, I operate on/in a system of cause and effect.

Theology, on the other hand is a look at the infinite, duration without beginning or end.

In order to handle this situation, I exercise the "Unknowable" function i.e., there is a veil behind which I cannot (at this time??) see; therefore, I cannot discern "initial conditions" (cause).

To get beyond this, I operate on the premise that "The Creator is the creation" and "The creation is the Creator".

To retain the vernacular, I call this phenomena "GOD".

As an aside: An analogy, if you will - As the Creator is the Creation, the organism man (I) is/am to my trillions of cells, and in this sense, "man is made in the image of "GOD"".

Given the above, in the beginning, GOD set the initial/starting conditions for the universe(s?).

From this point, we have Astrophysics, cosmology, astronomy, physics, science, religion and theology, not necessary in that order.

As this phase of the discourse is on theology (the above) and religion, I will now relate my (egotistical?) premise of religion.

Religion is a study and system of divining and acting on man's place after "The Beginning", and his/her relationship with GOD, the duties and activities demanded thereof, and how to insure that they will be done.

As and aside: I perceive that the very make up of "Higher" organisms allows/mandates them to have insights into that make up and therefore "know" what may be classified as "Unknowable", or in other words, realize some aspects of GOD (the creator/creation), Such as, as previously stated "man is made in the image of GOD". With this as a basis, I perceive that the only current divine intervention is some leakage of basic truths about the creation, into mans (my) consciousness. To complete the thought about intervention, I perceive that "GOD" does not "tweak" the system beyond that minor leakage of some basic truths, that are just emerging properties of our (my) gestalt organizational systems.

Back to religion – I perceive it as a carry over from the early beginnings of cognation in the Homo Line.

Not able to or willing to except that they were in control of their own destiny, they (we) set up and internal/external mental system.

They may have perceived that there were outside forces driving the environment and conditions around them, and personified them as anthro-beings that they may be able to appease in some manner.

I perceive that at first there were a multitude of these "beings", and as time progressed and culture/tradition became a larger part of the thinking process, this multitude took on the shape of sub-sets of greater beings, and as of now, for the most part, as a single mono GOD.

And finally, religious tenants seem to be methods to appease this GOD and to give him/her the mantel of good/evil, right/wrong etc., and to emulate these mantels for the betterment of man and men?

About GOD

As a beginning aside: I wrote this item before, in the first and second drafts of this discourse and edited it for the third draft. At the end of that edit while preparing to print the draft copy and clean up the manuscript file, I inadvertently deleted the original and the edited copy before I could print it.

Please note the above first statement, at the top of the page, and while you are reading the content of the following, wonder along with me, if I am in error to such an extent that a form of direct intervention took place and caused me to delete the files. I do/can not operate on this premise, so I am rewriting this section in/from the tenet of free will.

Before I start the rewrite I must comment more on the above.

This is not the first time that I have done the same thing to another file in the past, though a lack of attention (I think), or the possibility that I am just loosing it.

On another hand, as I have alluded to many times in this discourse, 80% of my thinking process is un/subconscious; so, I unconsciously may have deleted the file because I wasn't pleased with the content.

I know that none of the above may seem relevant; but, as this discourse is covering how I think, and in order to keep it truthful, I feel that I have no choice but to state the above aside.

With that said, I will now retype the vignette, with some more updating and editing that have come to mind during a very restless and long last night.

****

While doing this self analysis, I discovered that I needed to delve into the reasons behind myself and all the other selves, on and on, and the reason behind it all.

Why the universe, with all its hells and glory of creation and destruction of stars and galaxies?

Then the big question, why creation?

Although I am well aware of how finite and insignificant I am in relation to "The Big Picture", I am unable to stop myself from searching for the original cause and labeling it, and giving it a story.

Man is said to be a story teller, and I am a man with a story!

As I have stated before, I operate on the premise that there is a range of knowledge: the absolute unknown and unknowable, the unknown but knowable, and the known.

I will start with the absolute unknowable:

Behind this veil, I perceive and operate on the premise that there are creative forces. In says in the bible that GOD said: "I am the Alpha and Omega". I will call these forces the first two faces GOD, or the first two mansions (as in: Jesus said, "In my fathers house there are many mansions", or something along that line).

Next, the unknown but knowable:

I will take a page from Peirce and James, and take a leap of faith to find a pragmatic set of premises that work for me.

Behind this veil, I perceive and operate on the premise that there are also creative forces, perhaps subsets or extensions of the Alpha and Omega, that I call the other four faces of GOD, or the four other mansions.

I see these four faces of GOD, each mutually exclusive, yet of the same cloth, that define the operational creative forces of our universe(s?).

I will begin with the living GOD of the Old Testament, who created the heavens and the earth, and all the creatures there in, and gave man dominion over them, but remained involved and interactive with the creation and made/makes adjustments when necessary, to keep it on track: The Third Face of GOD?

Then I move on to the GOD of the Deists, who I believe (operate on the premise that) used the same creating process as The Third Face of GOD, but then after the creation, didn't/doesn't interact, but just watches/watched?: The Forth Face of GOD?

Then on to The Fifth Face of GOD, that I perceive is the GOD that the agnostics and atheists don't want to talk or think about. This GOD (creating force), may have looked upon the void and duplicated all his essence, but the divine, into a set of initial particles and conditions, placed then in a minute singularity and let the Big Bang happen; and then, like Elvis, left the building?

All of the above are viable pragmatic theories, but fall short of what works for me: the core of pragmatic thought.

Next, The Sixth Face of GOD: the creating force that I, in my pragmatic manner find more comfortable and workable.

In my pragmatic theory, this creating force consolidated the creative essence totally into the singularity, and became one with it, and after the Big Bang, the creator is the creation and the creation is the creator.

GOD; if you will, is part of me (US), and does not have to be an outside interacter or outside observer, or absent entity, but and intra-acter, within.

While I/we am/are an organism evolved from the Big Bang and subject to the Natural Laws incumbent to the initial conditions, there is a piece of the Creative Force within me (us) that can be reached and operated on/with (the leakage and/or emerging properties alluded to previously) under the right circumstances.

I perceive and operate on the premise that the right circumstances have to do with some facet of Free Will, which I covered in an earlier dichotomy. As goes the proper application of Free Will, so goes the intra-active process.

One last item or set of thoughts connected to/with the Creative Forces(s). Each Culture and/or Society or Religion uses mental and/or physical representations of this/these Forces. From my point of view, there are salient points in each and every different representation.

In some oriental views the numbers 5 and 8 are special. The 5 being a null or empty number (think of that point where a ball is thrown high in the air and goes up and up till it start down, the point between up and down is as the number 5), and the number 8 is infinity. In this arena, perhaps there is two more faces of GOD (mansions), the 7th: a transition or phase change between the Alfa and Omega and the 8th, a merging or the becoming infinite, while the number 5, the 5th face (the GOD of the atheist and/or agnostic?

In the Hindu Religion and/or lexicon, they use symbolic representations, such as Shiva. From what I have been able to gleam from the literature, there are several versions of the Shiva representation: A figure with 4, 6 or 8 arms.

Using what I have described above, I envision a Shiva representation standing on a nebula, with a back round of a spiral galaxy, with a sun or black hole at the end of each spiral. His head would consist of the six faces of GOD and he would have six arms; one for each face, one with the thumb pointing up (The Alpha) and one pointing down (The Omega), two with two thumbs and open hands, one with a closed fist with a cobra rapped around it, and the last hand open and held out in a friendly manner.

I am aware that I stretch a point here, but I am trying to say that each and every religion seems to have achieved some leakage that the others didn't, and maybe the same with individual organisms?

A final point, concerning philosophy and natural science:

Both allude to a spiritual property of the mind. Perhaps the evolution of this property allows/causes a different access to the spiritual?

Last, but not least: I don't find it hard to believe (operate on the premise that), the universe being infinite, from my perspective, the cliché – "What you see (a personal leap of faith) is what you get".

Finis

Early on I stated that after the dichotomies, I would write some vignettes on what I think about; but, since then I have found so many subjects I feel I need to white about, I will leave them for another complete work, so this is the end of my discourse.

Mini Bio

Family legend has it that I had a very traumatic birth. My mother was hemorrhaging badly and the young intern doing the procedure panicked, and while trying to extract me with his forceps, crushed my head like a prune and then threw me away in a wok like pan.

My Aunt Ethel; who was there, said that I put my hands on the edge of the pan and looked out, like Kilroy.

She picked me up and kneaded my head like bread dough, into a round ball as best she could. She didn't put her finger in my mouth and push out, so while most peoples' teeth are set at about 8", mine are about 26", so my profile is very flat and my nose is pugged.

The legend goes on to say that my first crib was the small top dresser drawer in my mother's bedroom.

I was born early and was very small, with a head full of bright red hair, that fell out and came back in black (almost navy blue) and as course as a horses tail.

I did not cry or make much noise until I was around three years old.

As the story goes, the little girl next door (Sarah?), was pounding Hires Root Beer caps into her fathers chopping block with a Boy Scout axe, and every time she would put one on the block to hit it, I would knock it off. She said if I didn't stop she would cut off my head. I didn't stop and she hit me in the head with the axe.

I supposedly ran into the house and talked or spoke for the first time - "Sarah hit me in the head with her has".

Some have said that I haven't stopped talking since.

The above was told to me by my Aunt Ethel over a quart of Jack Daniels Whiskey, while I was on leave from the Navy, in the early 50's.

She also told me that my father was a Navaho/Apache/Scotch half breed itinerant apple picker, who fell off our houseboat under the Ross Island Bridge in the Willamette River, in Portland Oregon, my home town, while drunk, and drowned, while I was very young.

His name was Harold Kellog, but as my mother was a free thinker and very liberal/liberated, in her three marriages, she never took her husbands name, but in her second marriage, she let her husband, John Morris Ironside, adopt me because he was the heir to a title in Scotland, and I might be have been able to come into it. I had a chance to go to Scotland for my education during World War II, but my mother was scared of the war, and didn't let me go, and that was the end of that.

Later when I had to get a Birth Certificate, it was registered under my mother's maiden name, so henceforth, I was called Robert Corron.

I am assuming that due to my birth trauma and the axe incident, my brain/mind and memory functions were curtailed... as I don't have any memories, except for in camera or cameo scenarios until just before my teens.

As an aside: I have heard and/or read that the cells in the body are replaced every 7 years or so, and that the brains neural cells set up new pathways if there is some damage to the old ones. So the following:

I remember nothing before I stated school, and little from then until after my thirteenth birthday, with more as I neared thirteen.

It seems that I was always smart (intelligent?), but ignorant/unaware and/or in the dark about a lot of things, and my attention span was pretty short and I would forget to do or not do this or that.

Hind sight (and a need for correlation and regression), tells me that I improved markedly during each 7 years following my teen years, until I was 42 years old and finally started and finished collage.

During the years 18 through 38 (about), I was a drunk and went through 2 marriages (my fault, both times I am sure?).

For what every reason, about 1970, I got (or my head got) my head straight and started life as a normal young adult (21) might.

I have since had a good professional career and a very successful 30 year marriage, until my wife died of Alzheimer's in 2000.

The above bio is only to highlight the beauty of the nature/nurture mix.

As an addendum, my birth trauma blurred some parameters of my thought process – I have spacial problems, as I may in some cases be two dimensional instead of three dimensional.

I was in collage before I realized that the Pythagorean theorem was not only linier but also spacial, and over 50 before I understood the exact ramification of the equal(=) sign in an equation.

Appendix 1

This is a List of My current Library, and is presented as acknowledgement to these authors for their input into my data base. This discourse is an extrapolation and innovation of these and all other media inputs.

Abbot, Edwin A. ,.Flatland

Azimov, Isaac .. The Relativity of Wrong

Barrow, John D. ..The Origin of the Universe

Barrow, John D. ..Theories of Everything

Bennett, Deborah J. .. Logic Made Easy

Brockman, John ..The Third Culture

Bryson, Bill ..The History of Nearly Everything

Casti, John L. ..Searching for Certainty

Damasio, Antonio ..Descartes Error

Damasio, Antonio ..Looking for Spinoza**

Damasio, Antonio ..The Feeling of What's Happening

Darwin, Charles ..The Descent of Man

Darwin, Charles ..The Origin of Species

Davies, Paul ..The last Three Minutes

Davies, Paul .. The Fifth Miracle

Davies, Paul ..The Cosmic Blueprint

Dawkins, Richard ..River out of Eden

Dawkins, Richard ..The Ancestors tale**

Dawkins, Richard ..The blind Watchmaker

De Duve, Christian ..Life Evolving, Molecules, Mind and Meaning

Dennett, Daniel ..Sweet Dreams**

Diamond, Jared .. Guns, Germs & Steel**

Diamond, Jared ..Collapse**

Edelman, Gerald M. & Tononi, Giulo .. The Universe of Consciousness**

Edelman, Gerald M. ..Bright Air, Brilliant Fire, and other Matters of Mind

Eldredge, Niles E. ..Why We Do It. Rethinking Sex and the Selfish Gene

Fernandez-Armesto, Felipe ..Human Kind, A brief History

Fernandez-Armesto, Felipe ..Ideas That Changed the World

Feynman, Richard P. .. Perfectly Reasonable Deviations*

Fischler, Martin A & Firschein, Oscar .. Intelligence

Gamov, George ..Mr. Thompkins in paperback

Gamov, George/Stannard, Leonard ..The new world of Mr. Thompkins

Gazzanica, Michael S. ..Mind Matters

Gee, Henry ..Jacobs Ladder

Gingerich, Owen ..The Eye of Heaven

Gladwell, Malcum ..BLINK, The Power of Thinking without Thinking

Gleick, James ..Chaos - Making a New Science

Gould, Stephen J. ..Bully for Brontosaurus

Gould, Stephen J. ..Dinosour in a Hay Stack

Gould, Stephen J. ..Eight Little Pigs

Gould, Stephen J. ..Ever Since Darwin

Gould, Stephen J. ..Hens Teeth and Horses Toes

Gould, Stephen J. ..I have landed

Gould, Stephen J. ..Leonadoes Mountain of Clams and the Dier of Clams

Gould, Stephen J. ..Ontogeny and Phylogeny*

Gould, Stephen J. ..Questioning the Millennium

Gould, Stephen J. ..Rock of Ages

Gould, Stephen J. ..The Flamingo's Smile

Gould, Stephen J. ..The Pandas Thumb

Gould, Stephen J. ..The Structure of Evolutionary Theory

Gould, Stephen J. ..Wonderful Life

Grant, John ..The Unsolved Mysteries of science

Green, Bryon ..The Fabric of the Universe

Gullies, Michael ..Bridges to Infinity

Halpern, Paul ..The Great Beyond

Hawking, Stephen .. A Brief History of Time

Hawking, Stephen ..Black Hole & Baby Universes

Hawking, Stephen ..The universe in a nut shell

Hawking, Thorne, Novikov, Ferris, Litman ..The Future of Space Time

Hawkins, Jeff ..On Intelligence

Johnson, Steven ..Mind Wide Open

Jones, Judy and Wilson, William ..The Incomplete Education

Jones, Steve .."Y" - The Descent of Man

Jones, Steve ..Darwin's Ghost

Kaku, Michio ..Parallel Worlds**

Koch, Kristof ..Quest for Consciousness

Kuttner, Paul ..Sciences Tricks & Questions

Laughlin, Robert B. ..A different Universe*

Leaky, Richard ..The origin of Human Kind

Lewin, Roger ..Complexity

Liber, Benjami ..Mind Time*

Mandler, Jean Matter ..The Foundation of Mind*

Mithen, Steven ..After the Ice*

Mock, Douglas W. ..More than Kin and Less than Kind

Morris, Concay ..Life's Solutions

Morris, Conway ..The Crucible of Creation

Muzar, Barry ..Imaging Numbers**

Nicolis, George & Ilya Prigogine ..Exploring Complexity

NYAC Volume 907 ..Evolutionary Perspectives on Human Reproductive Behavior

NYAS Volume 1000 ..Emotions inside out*

NYAS Volume 1001 ..The Self, From Soul to Brain

NYAS Volume 702 ..Brain Mechanics, In Memory of Robert Thompson

NYAS Volume 775 ..The Flight from Science and Reason

NYAS Volume 901 ..Closure

NYAS Volume 950 ..Quantum Questions

Penrose, Roger ..The Road to Reality*

Perkowitz, Sidney ..Digital People

Peterson, Ivers ..Fragments of Infinity*

Peterson, Ivers ..Newtons Clock, Chaos in the Solar System

Pink, Daniel ..A Whole New Mind*

Pinker, Steven ..How the Mind Works

Pinker, Steven ..The Blank Slate (The Modern Denial of Human Nature)

Pinker, Steven ..The Language instinct

Poundstone, William ..Prisoner's Dilemma - John Von Neuman, Game Theory ...

Ramachandran, V.S. ..A brief tour of Human Consciousness**

Rucker, Rudy .. Mind Tools - The Five Levels of Mathematical Reality*

Shapiro, Robert ..Origins, A Study Guide to the origins of life on Earth

Shermer, Michael ..Science of Good and Evil

Singh, Simon ..Big Bang, The Origins of the Universe*

Slobodkin, Lawerance B. ...Simplicity and Complexity in Games of the intellect

Smolin, Lee ..The Life of the Cosmos**

Spinoza ..Complete Works*

Stafford, Tom & Webb, Mathew .. Mind Hacks**

Stewart, Ian ..Flaterland

Thoreau, Henry D. ..Faith in a Seed

Tyson, Neil DeGrasse & Goldsmith, Donald ..Origins, Fourteen Billion...*

Ward, Finke & Smith ,,Creativity and the Mind, Discovering the Genius Within

Webb, Stephen ..Out of this World**

Wegner, Daniel M. ..The Illusion of Conscious Will**

Well, H.G. ..An Illustrated Short History of the World

Wilson, Edward O. ..Consilence, The Unity of Knowledge

Wilson, Edward O. ..Sociobiology

Yourgrau, Paul ..A World Without Time**

*Not yet read.

**Read or reading at after the discourse was written.

Not much different in general content, but some more detail and ambivalent semantics.

Appendix 2

(FIRST)

Start to see the day, and find a cloud,
Obscuring the view with dark shroud,
But, harken, a lining of silver threads,
And rays of colors billowing proud.

(2)

I am, therefore I think,
A mirror of Descartes?, I do not shrink,
From what I have found to be,
The Rosetta stone for me, and link.

(3)

And mighty sages do their bit,
And do their story with verve and wit,
Weave they prose's, true to form,
But, look, are they the writer, or the writ.

(4)

I have studied what they had to say,
And taken it as my own... nay,
But give them credit for all I use,
And add it to mine, each and every day.

(5)

I let my mind wander, to and fro
And to the winds let study go,
Each thing for me is new,
Even if it has been used by you.

(6)

I've been to see the elephant,
You've heard it said with cant,
By eleven blind scientist, each,
Having studied, from a different vant.

(7)

One at each and every leg,
They found it round as a keg,
All agreed, solid and firm,
But circular, with answers to beg

(8)

One to the trunk, with sheer delight,
Found it to be a fright,
Much like a snake, with scaly feel,
Would not stay, for fear of its bite.

(9)

Another to the tail, but found, alas,
Only a stick and a bunch of grass,
Sure he had lost his way,
He did not tell what had come to pass.

(10)

A pair to the ears, they studied that,
But found them only broad and flat,
They both agreed, not much to see,
Too thin and wide, and that was that.

(11)

On to the tusks, went two more,
And saw what none had seen before,
Found them solid and to the point,
Brand new ideas will go to the fore.

(12)

The last man, to our infinite regret,
Found a zebra, to study and pet
Very quadruped, small and common,
Is what he feels is what we get?

(13)

A sighted man, off to the right,
Saw all this, with sheer fright,
Stroking the zebra, white and black,
Will we accept this, without a fight?

(14)

A question arises, with the ameba,
Even Capricorn, Taurus and Libra,
And all beginnings, that we apprize,
Have we always stroked the zebra?

(15)

It been said, that there must be rules,
Secular or scientific, they are the tools,
They must be used, by one and all,
Are all who say this, philosophers or fools?

(16)

Each of the tasks must have their premises,
Or every conclusion, will be our Nemeses,
When we get to the end of the search,
Our reaction will always be grimaces.

(17)

When we are very young, we are said to toddle,
And as we become old, we then doodle,
What ever happens in the span of time,
In any and every case, we make of it a model.

(18)

When two of us perceive, we have a duality,
Our point of view, is not always reality,
There is a Core of vivid truth,
If this we do not see, then world wide futility?

(19)

There are five billion points of view,
And from our stand point, they are true,
But perceived reality, not the gold,
And to act upon it, may cause something new.

(20)

If it is core reality, that you wish to change,
In a precise manner, then operate on the same,
And do not act on perception only,
If you do, reaction will be out of your range.

(21)

In local situations, be aware of iso- this or that,
Regional coins have two sides, in fact,
Stay aware of this, for when all is the same,
If you meant to change, this is what you lack.

(22)

To analyze the future, we build a model,
Very much like a ship, in a bottle,
Be aware, it's not meant to float,
Or all your enterprise will topple.

(23)

A model is not reality, should not be,
But a tool to use, for you and me,
To put all the pieces in view,
Will it work, we must wait and see.

(24)

In theology, it is said, man is mud,
But in song, he is muscle and blood,
And the evolutionists say they,
Lo, it is silicate clays that bud.

(25)

There is a cosmos, our universe,
And a grand cosmos, that came first.
The universe, a process, random and open,
The grand cosmos, a force, more diverse?

(26)

Is the universe, liken to a cell,
A system, with inputs and outputs, well,
That sounds strangely, like it may live,
Does that mean it dies, and goes to hell?

(27)

Its now time to look at the solar system,
Before Copernicus, filled with mysticism,
Helo-centric, to say the least,
And now turns out, to be our prison?

(28)

To go even farther from the source,
Let's look at Earth, our only recourse,
A system, stable but open,
Our lovely haven, look with remorse.

(29)

From the heavens, a sparkling jewel,
But as an engine, it has limited fuel,
And we are using it, to a great degree,
As if the whole thing was run by a fool.

(30)

Complex and chaotic models, like economics,
Should make us look at thermo-dynamics,
If we don't realize the cost of entropy,
Our only result will be edomonics.

(31)

It is the nature of all social orders,
Invariable it seems, to insist on borders,
If within your border, you cannot sustain,
And have no surplus, you will belong to others

(32)

Why must we always, seek our success?
As if a single factor, explanation to address,
Will assure, that we do not fail,
When to eliminate causes of failure is best.

(33)

I often get a yen, for the world of Venn,
I see the Complement, and then,
All else, must be what I seek
And from this point begin?

(34)

There is a place, very hard to fathom,
Standing between the physical and quantum
Between probability and reality,
That may allow RNA/DNA to do what HE wantem.

(35)

In the world of quantum mechanics,
As in music, are there harmonics?
That allows the same message to multiply,
a complexity lacking in economics?

(36)

When you think gravity, is it really a graviton,
That you are trying to put your finger on,
Is there a clue to the attractive glue?
That is causing the changing Model marathon?

(37)

Our sub-atomic models are very complex,
Is adding new levels, in context,
Or have we lost sight of Oakum's razor,
The tool to keep us from reflex?

(38)

And the Universe was born from a seed,
And was it done out of need,
For the model of an onion,
And if so, might we best take heed?

(39)

And the Universe was layered in Planes,
And the Planes separated by planes,
For they were separate, but joined
And all things are used again and again?

(40)

And the Planes were two layers of net,
And each body fit inside, you bet,
For as they grew the net spread,
And waves of light follow the lines yet?

(41)

And it was that there was a bud, not connected
And impendent, but protected,
For our onion is alone, not as we would like
But drifting from where it was ejected?

(42)

And it was that the planes were powered
And power, gravity, not to be cowered,
For when the net of the Plane stretched,
And it did with mass, gravitons showered?

(43)

And black holes, it was that recycled gravity,
And from the Plane back to the plane rapidly,
For the Universe is a process, open and random,
And those who will not see, suffer depravity?

(44)

And it is visualized, by an analogy,
And this, without apology,
For fractals, by definition, can represent,
And all things being equal, knowledge?

(45)

And a fish net, layered, hanging high
And glass floats in between, nigh
For there must be a visual bump
And now you can see the light waves hump?

(46)

And it has been found, logic has no truth
And from false premise, there is no worth
For if a thing is right, for the wrong reason
And if used again, it ends in still birth?

(47)

If I find the right answer, for the wrong reason
I may find myself, committing treason
There is no truth in a solution
That follows logic from a bad conclusion

(48)

And by the very logic I eschew,
And by this logic, I can prove it true
For Fractal/morphology/sameness/representation,
And representation to fractal... can't you?

(49)

What is it that separates man?
Is it his ability, to plan?
To project the future, by extension,
And is it proven, that only he can?

(50)

We use the language, as a tool,
But out of context, we are a fool,
Be aware of the subject, at the time,
So that you may always, keep your cool.

(51)

To be at one, with the universe,
We must be able, to converse,
With Yang and Yin, balanced and whole
Or our response will be perverse.

(52)

There are connections, far and near,
That we strive to reach, and hold dear,
We search for those that will make us rich
And from the success of others, we mirror.

(53)

In the East, they seem to nurture,
Not benevolent, but feudal culture
In the West, momism, and the consumer
Is it a nanny corps, or a vulture.

(LAST)

To begin is to set a path to the end,
And no matter what rules, this we cannot fend,
We have started a string of thoughts,
So later or ever we will not pend?

Part Two

WHAT DO I THINK ABOUT

FROM A TO Z

Contents

Dedication Page

I dedicate this project to the John and Lynn McCoy, my neighbors.

We met and became neighbors and friends after I sold then some land next door, while I was working on my previous project i.e., "How and why do I think as I do".

It became very obvious, very rapidly that our political views were different.

The McCoy's are left of center and I am right of center, to say the least.

We meet in the middle on most facets of civil rights, but in most other areas we are poles apart.

The McCoy's are academics, school teachers and in the case of John, also an athletic coach.

Contrary to what one might think, our differences of opinion have strengthened the bonds of our relationship.

We both feel free to express our point of view and debate their various attributes.

The main reason for this dedication is that through our various discourses, I have had to reanalyze my knee jerk, canned reactions to their various points of view, and modify my negation of their ideas.

This project was to be about what I think and what I think about and I started it, even in conception, after our association began.

As the friendship and relationship grew, so did the project.

Through our various exchanges and/or debates I was forced, to my own edification, to reanalyze the data I was or had been using to make decisions on various political situations, and to examine more closely my parochial biases.

As seems to be the norm, from my perspective at least, many of my ideas and operating premise were based on incomplete, thin, partial, or a complete lack of pertinent data.

In a word, they forced me to actually think about situations instead of just reacting on preconceived and often outdated data.

My self and this project are better due to our relationship.

If I ever reach maturity, enlightenment, or become one with the Universe, the McCoy input will have been a prime factor.

Preface

This project is about what I think and what I think about.

The alphabetic format is an arbitrary presentation of subjects in this journal that covers most of my thinking process.

Each section or subject should be able to stand alone and/or be a continuation or addition/amendment to one of the other sections.

In some cases my parochial bias may be prevalent, while in other I will try to overcome these tendencies and present the data in a reasonable objective matter and not as a rationalization of preconceived or incomplete ideas?

In some cases they may just be prediction or even fantasy.

If you find some question marks on/in some statements, they are there because I question the thought and/or think that you, the reader might wish to question is also.

Post Script

I realize that the Post Script usually follows the body of a given presentation, but in this case I feel that is should come at this time.

My intent at the beginning of this project was to delineate what I thought about, in a self analyzing manner.

That was and is not the case.

The result is iconoclastic.

I had and have no intent to deride the creating forces, or in the vernacular, GOD.

I do find myself; however, deriding the many things that man has done and is doing in the name of GOD, Christ, Mohammed and any or all other facets of the GODHEAD.

So the iconoclastic jousting is not aimed at religious or political entities, but at the men who have, and still are using these entities to the detriment of the various societies, cultures, governments, and for all practical purposes, the entire world.

You, the reader, will note that I am a Deist, who operates on the premise that the perfect GOD, or the creating force, in my lexicon, set the Cosmos in motion in such a manner that there was or will be no need to change or interact with the creation.

Abortion

By definition to abort (stop) a process.

Definition for this project: to abort a human fetus.

There are several types of abortion:

> Miscarriage – from natural causes
> Miscarriage – from physical abuse
> Miscarriage – from lack of natal care

These above abortions don't receive much attention, comment or controversy.

The abortion that I will comment on here is, in the vernacular, labeled pro-choice vs pro-life.

Pro-choice: the right to choose weather or not to carry a fetus to term vs pro-life: the elimination of this option, for all practical purposes.

Abortion is not new. It has long been a part of (at least) the human life style.

For the most part, there has been an economic cost function operation is this area, both in the human and other animal species.

It doesn't seem to have been much of a social issue until the Judaic/Christian era.

Also, during the period of King's right, that tradition that allowed the clan leader to bed each new bride before the husband, on the wedding night, abortion was no allowed for that first child.

After the Catholic Church dominated most European societies, abortion became illegal in those societies, and this trend was carried over to the colonies from England.

Although abortion was illegal in the United States, there was not a wide spread controversy until the Supreme Court decision in Roe v Wade that established the right to choose.

I will focus on what I think I know about the abortion issue in the United States, since Roe v Wade.

From what I understand, the Supreme Court placed Pro-choice under the umbrella of the bill or rights and that the Pro-life faction, the Catholic Church has preached against it, and the right wing conservative Christians and fellow travelers have tried to overturn the Supreme Court decision.

I have a personal propensity toward the pragmatic, that philosophy that advocates what works for me, or for you, as long as what works for you is not in my space, and/or a focus on the economic, therefore "choice" is high on my list of priorities.

In the case of abortion; from my point of view, it is ladies choice, as it should be in all male/female relationships.

I perceive that the pro-life arguments have three basic foundational ideas:

> (1) Old Testament Religion
> (2) Criminal (murder)
> (3) Psychological

From the Old Testament Religion point of view, I perceive that:

> (6) Go forth and inhabit the earth. (done?)
> (7) No self induced death or suicide. Abortion as suicide inflicted on the unborn.
> (8) Life begins at conception
> (9) The sex act is for procreation only and not pleasure and in the eyes of GOD, to abort a child is an abomination.

From the Criminal (murder) argument (2) above indicates that abortion is murder.

From the Psychological point of view, the mother who aborts her child will feel forever guilty, even if she doesn't realize it.

The Pro-choice rebuttal, from my point of view, of the above is as follows:

> (1) I am a deist, and when you take the interactive god out of the equation there is no abomination.
> (2) Life begins at birth, when the umbilical cord is cut and the mother no longer provides the life force.
> (3) With out the Old Testament beliefs there would be no No guilt, therefore no psychological problems.

Behavior

By dictionary definition:

The manner in which on behaves, deportment, demeanor or the actions or reactions of persons or things under specified circumstances.

The purpose of this section is to delineate and/or define why my behavior is such that it is.

I am sure that I am not absolutely unique in my behavioral patterns, but I am forced, through observation of the reactions of most others, that in this area, at least, the Deme is very small.

This journal is about what I think – an extension of the previous "How and why do I think as I do?", so my behavior is a synthesis of how I think and what I think.

The question, then, is, why do I behave as I do?

Consider the basic instincts of "R", the old, reptilian, lower part of the brain, associated with my parochial bias, that data laid down early in life, possibly, according to the psychologists, before I was five years old, but at least prior to the teen years, coupled with the unconscious processing, that 80% of the pre-cognitive process, associated with the 20% override of the pre-frontal cortex, in conjunction with the free will that is also exercised in that pre-frontal cortex 20%.

Given the above, with what the functions of nature and pre-natal nurture, environmental inputs, such a parenting, status, location, rural or urban, rich or poor and last but not least diet, as you are what you eat?

Added to the previous are, social constraints at the family, community and governmental levels, and my individual reactions to these constraints e.g., rebel or comply, or some synthesis of both.

Unless one does more than suffer through Psyc101, these questions and/or arguments may not come up, as in my case, until a certain level of maturity has been reached.

Once I even thought about my behavior or behavioral patterns and then compared them to my compatriots, I found that there were some facets that were not only contradictory, but also uncomfortable, when contrasted with the behavior of those contemporaries.

What I think or thought, in the areas of social interaction, once highlighted, turn out to be very hard to modify to comply with my new level of maturity.

Because of this I have become more forgiving of the parochial bias in my peers.

Life goes smoother if I just let it go.

Compultion

The dictionary defines compulsion as an irresistible impulse to act in a certain way regardless of the rationality of the motivation.

It also defines Impulse as a sudden inclination or urge, a desire or whim, a motivating propensity, a drive, an instinct.

And also defines motivation as the mental process, function or instinct that produces and sustains incentive or drive in human or animal behavior.

It seems to me, here, that we have a classic case of semantic non-closure; that is the three definitions allude to several different mental states or explicit brain areas and/or functions.

For instance, instinct, that behavioral function that is related to "R", the old reptilian or hind brain, that initiates the fight or flight complex.

It also allude to rationality, a mental function, by definition, that is a pre-conceived goal oriented operation that only uses data points that fulfill or at least lead toward that goal.

And then impulse, a propensity: by definition, an innate inclination, tendency or bent, plus as an added aside, an act that I repeated over and over again, when a certain set of circumstances arise; and inclination, again propensity, urge, and unconscious drive, a desire, a goal driven assumed need and finally a whim, a snap judgment, caused by unconscious processes without pre-frontal cortex modification; that is there is no exercise of the free will function to negate the unconscious process with conscious thought.

I could go on defining each and every word/concept in the above, but I hope you get the point.

What we think and do is part and parcel of how we think.

This section is dedicated toward the idea that in order to think and/or act in a reasonable manner, that is to follow the data to its conclusion without a pre-conceived goal, I must have semantic closure.

I must know the meanings of words in context, in it self a marvel of the cognitive process.

Corrons' Dialectic Polyhedron

A review; perhaps not for the reader, but as a starting point for this section.

The simple dialectic starts with a thesis, a certain point of view that is then placed in a dichotomy in contention with an antithesis, another point of view covering the same subject.

Through various combinations of analysis and compromise, a new entity is born, synthesis.

Therefore you have a thesis that may have been the synthesis of a prior dialectic process, an antithesis that also may have been the synthesis of another process, and again another synthesis.

Thesis, antithesis, synthesis: what a concept; perhaps, from my point of view, the most important idea that the species has ever come up with.

That's enough of the dialectic primer, now on to the meat of this section.

In evolution biology theory there is a model for an if then do loop called Galtons' Polyhedron, in which at a given point in a process, the next step may be one of several or no change at all.

How this can be visualized is the next point.

Assume a process, slowed down to such a state that it was static and discrete i.e., all the individual pieces, parts and process are frozen in time.

From a linier point of view, then the process may go forward one step at a time.

Picture a node with multiple branches, each branch, to the next step to the process, depending on what one of many addition or deletions to the process is/was chosen.

From the point of view of the polyhedron idea, the next step in the process could be no change, move one step forward in the same direction, otherwise, if he polyhedron rolls over to any one of the faces connected to the starting face, then whatever action that face indicated was/is the next step or direction of movement.

As can be seen, although there can be some movement or change of movement of the process, it is limited to the faces congruent to the starting point, that is any change at any step would be very small at each discrete phase.

Over a long period of time or through a multiple of many steps and then to go forward with no change, called static evolution, or to roll over to other faces of the polyhedron to continue the evolution process.

In this case, it can be seen that the outcome would be deterministic because the number of faces is fixed, but not predestined, due to the multiple ways each choice could cause/allow the process to go.

This was originally a modeling tool, I perceive, to describe natural selection and the environmental niche process for evolution.

I may have interpreted the data correctly or misinterpreted it to fit my limited grasp on the subject; however, I will carry on anyway.

The above is not the real point here. All I am trying to do is to use the polyhedron idea to show that there may be a multiple of antithesis and the possible and synthesis may have a very broad range.

A point is that even though the dialectic may be one of the most important mental tool that has ever been discovered or conceptualized, one can spin the antithesis and therefore the synthesis.

A caution: just because a model of a process or even the process it self shows great promise, I must remember that the step from pure reason to goal oriented rationality is just one face away. Beware!

Deme

Deme; the root word, from my prospective, of demographics —Sub societies, groups, people of the same bent, culture and sub cultures.

In this section I am dealing with the many of which I may be one.

A deme is therefore the label I place on a group that have more in common than not, and that have a tendency to act in accord, given a certain stimulus.

Please notice that I stated that they had more things in common than not, witch indicates that even though statistically one might be able to predict the probability of a certain result or output, given a specific stimulus or input, this is still just a statistical probability and not cut in stone.

One can, more or less depend on the outcome if the deme is large enough and the stimulus input is precise enough.

The direction I am going here is to point out that most individuals, in most cases, most of the time, will react mostly the same as the rest of their deme.

Please note that I did not say the most individuals, most of the time will be decent, moral or ethical, from ones point of view most of the time.

By the very nature of human nature, demes, sub demes, supra demes, what ever manner of scale you overlay them with, have different cultural traditions, social foundations, broad differences on how to act in a given situation, and I am sorry to say, a different interpretation of the word of their particular version of the interactive god.

The founding fathers of the United States knew well this state of affairs from their acute and precise study and understanding of the previous results of states that combine the religious with the political.

The very foundations of our constitutional government are clear that there had to be a complete separation between church and state.

I a word, in order for the enlightened state to exist, it had to operate under the precise laws laid down by men, and not the arbitrary laws laid down from the various laws laid down by the various religions, in the name of their various (but the same??) interactive god.

A an important aside, the specie, us, humans, also will only continue to exist if they learn to operate in the same manner as the enlightened state that the founding fathers perceived.

I have said this before and probably will say it gain, the founding fathers, who I perceive as having been Deists, put "In GOD We Trust" on the national seal because they meant that GOD in his perfection, created the creation, and that they trusted that he would/will not interfere or interact with his own perfection.

I know that it seems I have again wandered from my subject, but bear with me and I may be able to clarify the above in the context of this section?

There are a number of individuals in each and every deme that fall out of the definition of most individual, most of the time.

These individuals, although in the minority in each deme may form a new sub deme of those who don't just go alone, but try to reason through a given situation.

This deme may be the savior of the species, but my fatalist bent causes me to even doubt this chance for survival.

We will need a lot of cooperation to put ourselves in a position to get off this rock before the sun cooks us.

Only that sub deme, the minorities, the independent, those reasoners, can put us in a position to find a way to survive.

Demons – Psycic Impulses

Although I was not consciously aware of any special subject order in my alphabetical list compiled for this project, I may have unconsciously listed Behavior, Compulsion and Demons in the order present.

"DEMONS" is my personal label for those broken or bent psychological agents that upset, or have the potential to upset my normal psychological states.

This section does not or is not intended to cover psychotic breakdown, such as schizophrenia, paranoia, or polar issues, but those demons; despair, despondency and depression.

First, despair, that often panic driven, at least in my case, temporary feeling of loss of control of the situation, a sinking feeling that causes my normal conscious process to falter and become disoriented.

Personally, I feel that this is the doorway to all the other demons, and if not contained, can or will lead to the other two demons, and/or beyond, to major psychic breakdown.

In my case, I find that despair can be controlled with a pause to relax and take a few deep breathes and bring my mind to another subject.

I strongly feel that if I don't alleviate the despair, that I would/will fall further into despondency and depression.

So far in my life, I have been fortunate to be able to calm my temporary despair before it becomes despondency or depression.

However, I perceive that if I did not try and succeed to overcome despair, I would have fallen through to despondency and depression.

Here's where the "What I Think" part comes in.

As I stated often in "How and Why Do I Think as I Do", if I slip into the vernacular and say 'I think' or 'I believe' or 'disbelieve', what I am really trying to say is that 'I operate on the premise that' what ever the subject at hand.

Continuing may train of thought, I operate on the premise that, if a person, myself or others in my deme, allow themselves through the door of despair, they will fall into the arms of despondency and depression.

My point in all this is that I may, because of uncontrolled despair, force the door open to the other demons.

I am the master of my fate, as long as I don't scratch the scab of despair and force the door open.

Discrete And/0r Continuous

When I think about discrete and continuous, I often relate them to digital and analogue, but this can sometimes muddy the waters.

I this section I will try , at least for my own edification, to unravel or clean up any of those complex issues that may have become more complicated than necessary, in relation to Discrete and/or Continuous.

The term discrete, for the purposes here, does not have anything to do with one being talking about the activities of, usually shady, others.

The discrete that I am thinking about here has to do with individual objects in a state of isolation and static motion.

If I am thinking about a discrete object, I am not thinking about the previous or following object, or what type or category of the object, but just that object itself.

What does it imply, now, in this situation, and relation to me, at this time?

The object I am thinking of or about will not be connected with the duration of that object, because it will have none.

The temporal aspect of a discrete object or this particular object I am thinking of is nil.

This is not to say the a discrete object or event or the object I am thinking of did not have a prior position in the universe or would/

will not have another position or status in the future, only that when I am observing the discrete, item, event, object, number, or what ever individual entity I am observing, or postulating, is motionless, static, frozen in time, alone and observable in real time and/or reality or just in conjecture.

What I mean by conjecture is in reference to things like numbers, you cannot see a number, just the symbol that represents it in a semiotic, coded manner.

A discrete moment in a process or system finds the entire system or process at a complete standstill, but I am not interested at any one time on more than one discrete entity in or of that system or process.

For instance, I think of an automobile accident at an intersection is a good example of explaining the discrete function.

I wish to choose or find the last discrete moment that the accident could have been prevented.

The individual item, event, or entity, involved are a package of all discrete entities and are collectively analyzed from the point of view of each of their discrete positions at that last instant that the accident could have been avoided, and what discrete events lead up to that last discrete moment, frozen, static, in time.

Scenario: Car "A" is entering the intersection at the instant that the light changes from yellow to red.

Car "B" is traveling down the cross street and either doesn't see car "A", or the red light, or both, and enters the intersection and broadsides car "A".

The discrete moment I am looking for is that moment when the driver of car "A" could have seen that car "B" was going too fast in time to prevent the accident or when the driver of car "B" should have observed the actual situation and slowed down and stopped, even though at the moment he would enter the intersection the light would be green.

Just a short time, seconds/split seconds, car "B" could not stop the accident. By definition, the driver of car "A" should have observed that car "B" was going to fast to stop in time, and not run the yellow light.

I am aware that that long drawn out written observation took more time than the event described.

There is no duration in a discrete event, although it is still temporal, in the time line, it is frozen.

The observer, who mentally freezes time, to observe the discrete moment, has duration and moves through or down the time line, even though the imagined discrete moment is static.

A discrete instance/item is frozen in time, as a number standing alone in a discrete situation is not involved with the continuous flow of that particular set of numbers, but only the number itself.

6 is my favorite number, a discrete 6 is only an abstract, semiotic, coding devise that fixes its attributes between 5 and 7, but tells me nothing about 6 itself.

As with the car accident, you have to expand the discrete entity to encompass the set of all other items involved in the situation you are trying to analyze.

With 6, is it apples, seconds, quarks, life times or what ever?

It is a discrete moment in time, of and entity, along with all its connecting attributes that make analysis possible

It still may seem muddy, but in a word, discrete events are frozen moments in the continuous processes and activities of life and time.

The reason this is important to what I think about, is that any and/ or every discrete moment in my life I have one or more choices at what to do next.

There is nothing I can do about past decisions except to try to learn from the bad ones, but in planning the future I can enter a mental do loop, that is, in a given situation if this is so, then do this i.e., if then do, or breaking it down further into discrete logical notation, if and only if, then do.

My entire life and future, and perhaps the future of those close to me, depends the decisions I make from one discrete moment to the next.

Back to the subject of this section, a continuous good life depends on the right response to each discrete decision point.

Environment And Environmental Decline

This sections' subject will be presented in a dialectic manner, pro, con, conclusion and discourse.

It will cover not only physical environmental issues; but also, cultural evolution and/or changes in both during the last half century.

The pro/con discussion will cover global warming, its causes, effects and possible solutions.

First, the pro – yes we are seeing a noticeable increase in global temperatures.

The blame is presently, mainly being laid at the feet of the increase of green house gases that in turn is being laid at the feet of human intervention.

Second, the con – Yes we are seeing a noticeable increase in global temperatures and green house gases, but the burning of fossil fuels and other human activities are too insignificant when compared with the entire earth system of equilibrium and the cycles of warming and cooling.

Conclusion – yes we are in a state of global warming.

Here's the rub; while both sides of the argument agree on global warming, neither can agree on a working solution to the problem.

Now, that that part is presented, I wish to discourse on the other aspects of this situation.

It doesn't matter who is right about the causes of global warming.

What we should be looking at what effect this is having on the air quality and other atmospheric conditions.

We had a glimmer of reason when it was discovered that the ozone layer was thinning over Antarctica and elsewhere.

It was discovered that the CFC's from spray cans and Freon from heating and cooling devises was a main cause, and we, the collective global community did something about it. We curtailed the use of these products.

As an aside, the DDT spray was about the same. While DDT was the best pest control chemical mix ever found, it has side effect of thinning the membranes around every kind of egg, causing a drastic reduction in the reproduction capabilities of fish and fowl and even the potential for doing the same thing to other mammals and the human specie.

Once again the global community was able to put in place systems to alleviate the situation.

My main point of view, here, is that the global community can and does something about environmental situations when there is a consensus of the cause, effect and cure.

As to global warming, even though all parties agree that it is happening, there is no solid consensus of how the problem should be addressed.

I operate under the perception that the wrong problem is being discussed.

Health issues of humans and other life form on our earth should be the main concern when discussing the atmospheric pollution with green house gases or what ever.

It can be understood by all, that the current usage of fossil fuels around the world is causing air pollution that if continued, will lead us all to extinction.

If the global community gets a handle on controlling pollution, the immediate result well be in the health area, and if human intervention is indeed connected to global warming, that area also.

There should be a system put in place, at the global level, to use available technology to insure less pollution, conservation, recycling and alternate sources of energy.

A lot of these things are being done, without any collective sharing of ideas and or methods that are working.

This could be something that the UN could do instead of always being behind the power curve i.e., peace keeping instead of war stopping.

And last but no least, the world cannot sustain the current population trends much longer.

As each third world country raises their collective standard of living the drain on limited resources will increase.

The only solution to this is to freeze or reduce population growth or best case, reduce the population.

If we don't, nature is going to do it for us through pandemic episodes and/or the Paris sewer rat syndrome.

Case in point, we have known about HIV/AIDS for over 20 years, but it is still running rampart around the world, and in addition those people infected have weakened immune systems that are perfect breeding grounds for any pandemic agent.

We have come a long way in the medical area of this problem, but are really only doing lip service to a real solution. The only gains, or at least viable attempts to alleviate this situation are being driven by the few in the private sector that have enough money to do some good.

This is not going to cut it. Governments in unity and the UN are going to have to get their act together and face up to the issue that they are not accomplishing much with their infighting over political and religious matters.

Another facet of population control is being attained by the international terrorist organizations.

While this is fact reduces the population, I don't think it is a viable answer to the problem.

But, rather abruptly brings me to the next level of the Environmental/ Evolutionary situation.

Our cultural environment has changed immensely in the last half century.

We have at least doubled the number of sovereign states, and within these state there are multicultural tensions.

In many sovereign states, there is a fundamentalist Muslim state or shadow government.

This appears to be the result of the Saudi Arabian missionary activities over the last few decades. They sent missionaries around the world to convert the poor and suppressed in the third world to

Islam, and in some cases absorbing the remnants of lost Marxists causes.

It seems; however, from my point of view, that the only clerics that went on these missions were fundamentalists, in the majority. Whether this was the intent of the missions in the first place, they seem to have turned out to be the seedbeds of international terrorism?

The above is just one change in our cultural situation.

From the American prospective, outsourcing has caused or allowed another cultural shift, in that with many jobs being sent overseas, population growth and uncontrolled migration are causing new social tensions.

There is a lot of talk about illegal immigration, but I don't hear much about the real problem, from my point of view.

To put the above, and what follows on perspective, I feel I must go into some controversial areas, mainly, the capabilities and limitations of the individual and his/her deme.

Deme: by definition, that grouping of people who are very much alike, in most cases, most of the time. (See the previous section on DEME).

My first scenario will start with the service/computer revolution starting in the last sixties and culminating in the late nineties and continuing today.

Prior to this event the main service areas, in the non professional, were teaching, food service, office help, some common labor and care giving.

Although nurses were highly trained and competent, they were still considered in the service realm, rather than the professional i.e., doctors, lawyers and accountants.

This is because the demes, from the point of view of our society, are divided by levels (class?) of competence, and/or value, real or perceived.

With this leveling in mind, I visualize that the most competent demes, out side the professional ranks, migrated to those areas mentioned above.

I think about the fact that sometime ago sales people, waiters, waitresses, bartenders, busboys/girls and all other personal contact people were more polite and did a better and more competent job with a much better overall attitude than now.

I operate on the premise (perceive/think) that this change (evolution) is caused, or at least attributed to by the opening up of computer related jobs to those higher level demes, that in the past had filled the personal contact and/or service jobs, leaving those areas without the best demes of the non professional labor pool.

As an aside, it has been said that we all are created equal and have the same opportunity to achieve, but I note that we all do not have the same capabilities and limitations.

As the service jobs had to be filled, next lower or highest remaining deme peculated up to fill these positions and services they supplied suffered accordingly do to the relative change in the capabilities and limitations of the individual and/or deme.

Case in point, it used to be more difficult to get into nursing school than it is now, plus the fact that there are less applicants applying and that there are less training facilities, and as the population is increasing, there is a dearth of nurses being trained in the United States.

Although hospitals are recruiting nurses from overseas, there is still a shortage that is being replaced by health/care givers with less than one year training.

This is just one example of a deme peculating up to the next level of service. I am sure the reader can plug in more occupations that have the same scenario.

Although there is no regression with the correlation that since this trend started, hospital fatalities per capita have increased.

Current published data indicates that this is lack of continuity in standardization of certain procedures and that MRSA is on the increase.

It seems possible to me the less trained and lower demes, from janitors thru administrators, associated with hospitals may be part of the problem, along with the economic environments of many rural hospitals that are not up to par.

This, as an aside, correlates with the economic environment throughout the country that has allowed the entire infrastructure to fall into disrepair.

With that said, I will go back to outsourcing and some further ramifications.

As jobs are being outsourced to second and third world countries, their standard of living is increasing, adding to the demand for more energy recourses, putting more pressure on supply, that is slowly, and sometimes not so slowly, causing the price of oil to increase.

It has been predicted since the 1950's that the oil supply was not unlimited and would someday run out.

With the rise of the second and third world countries, that run out may accrue faster then even the most conservative estimates.

This just reemphasizes the need for more research and implementation of alternate energy resources.

Along with this issue, the law of conservation comes into play; nothing in the systems of nature is lost, just turned into something else.

When I got this idea, I asked my self what's the connection?

Well, given that the total resources available on this earth are limited, and the second and third world countries are needing more, it stands to reason the first world countries will have less.

As stated above, the second and third world countries are seeing a raise in their standard of living, it goes hand in hand that the first world countries will loose a proportion of their standard of living to comply with the laws of conservation.

An example of this is becoming evident with the jobs being created in this country to replace the outsourced positions.

For the most part these new jobs don't pay as much as the ones that they have replaced.

This is bound to have an effect on the standard of living for those people involved.

Another trend that is starting, in that some people are following the jobs and moving to second and third world countries; where although the salaries are less, the living expenses are also less, so their standard of living does not decrease as much, and in some cases increases from what they had here.

In addition, this is also adding to brain drain.

On another hand, with outsourcing, the deme levels that I spoke about earlier now have movement in the other direction.

Higher qualified people are now vying for the remaining jobs, and getting them, which in turn causes the removed deme, which is more qualified than the one below, to replace them.

Now, I perceive that some readers may think that I am over stating the qualification difference between my alluded demes.

I would suggest that they look closely at the illegal immigration situation.

It is assumed, by the talking heads in the media, that the illegals are hired by companies because they have jobs that must be done, that the current U.S. work force will not do for the wages that the companies must pay to stay competitive.

As an aside, one may look at this as circular, due to the fact that the competing companies may be saying the same thing?

The immigration acts of the late eighties temporarily alleviated the situation, but in the last twenty years it has gotten out of hand to the point that the problem is being debated heavily at both the federal and lower levels.

Looking at this situation from another aspect, one may see that the underbelly of laissez faire capitalism raising it ugly head.

Case in point, big companies who utilize these illegals (who all have false *I.D.'s?) keep the wages low* because the illegals can't afford to make a wave.

Now, you add the downward pressure of the deme movement, and you get legals that will do these tough jobs.

I perceive that from the point of view of the companies involved, they must do anything they can to stop any legislation that would stop the flow or reduce in any manner their illegal work force.

If they don't, and they have to hire legals, they would loose their leverage in a union situation, and risk the possibility that the new employees will force them to raise wages and benefits.

This will in turn increase the costs to the consumer, which goes back to my earlier point, reduce their standard of living and also inhibit our ability to compete with the overseas buyers and sellers.

I know that this is a broad stretch from my starting premise on this subject, but after I got started, it just got a life of its own and wrote itself.

I am sure that further on down the line I will revisit and look into some of the above areas and think more about them.

Fear

Fear: The Emotion
Fear: The political Tool
Fear: The Psychological Paranoia
Fear: The Terrorist Tool
I (we) have the potential for fear.

At the dawn of human evolution, it was probably the key emotion to survival i.e., fight or flight.

The entity; man or beast, that allowed fear to cause it to run away and fight another day, did survive that particular situation, but the entity that controlled the fear, often stood its ground and eliminated the cause of the fear.

The correct mix of these activities was part of the selection process that produced more offspring and perpetrated the specie.

Some time during the growth of civilization, the first spin doctors began to utilize fear as a tool, either for internal political or religious reasons, or for external reasons i.e., the threat of war on their neighbors.

I am assuming that paranoia is a late bloomer, in that it is probably an epigenic (Nurture) result of a more polluted environment and a more complex social order?

This is just an assumption, reverting back to my previous project, "How and Why Do I Think As I Do".

The reason for the above preamble is to have laid the ground work for the reason I included this subject/section in this work.

As stated, this work is about what I think, and it follows, what I think about.

If I haven't made it clear before, the entire work is based on my personal observation of the current world situation, filtered through my deepest unconscious parochial bias's and the entire data base of my personal experiences, modified by everything I have read, heard and/or received as input from what ever media concerned.

To round this out, one of my basic operation premises rests on the 80/20 hubristic.

80% of my mental activity is unconscious, channeled to the pre-frontal cortex, where the final 20% of the cognitive process and free will cause/allow/control my final conclusion/decision.

That last series of caveat was to show that what I present here, in this and the previous project, is what I think (my operating premise), there is meant no assurance that my observations and conclusions have any relevance to core reality.

I'll say this again; I try to operate in the philosophical mode at all times: I believe or disbelieve nothing, because I am finite and the available, and unavailable, data is infinite, so I don't ever have a complete grasp on reality and never know the truth, or at least the whole truth. I know that I cannot function in this manner, so I use operating premises to replace the concepts: 'I think' or 'I believe'.

These premises are very fluid and change with whatever the situation is, and/or what ever new data is added to the mix.

It is not outside their function to sometimes be contradictory or fuzzy.

I have alluded to this premise based functionality many times in my previous work: "How and Why Do I Think As I Do", and in the preface of this project, and will probably reiterate it again and again, because the subject/sections presented here can and should be able to stand alone and also be part of the whole, and if the premise based functions are relevant to the subject, they will be included.

This redundancy may seem overdone, but I use it like math and spelling drills are used to make sure the object/subject is locked into long term memory and is easily recovered and/or remembered, and used when appropriate. I hope you, the reader can and will bear with me on this?

Enough of the machinery of this project; now back to FEAR.

FDR said "We have nothing to fear except fear itself".

I am trying to operate within this statement.

In the current state of world religion, politics, diplomacy and war, what function is fear following?

As I have stated earlier, one of my main focuses is economics and its/their ramifications.

What is the focus of my various fears on the economic front, in the world view, from local economics to global economics?

Starting with religion, the economics, except for fund raising, don't seem to be an obvious large part of the equation, but fear at some or several levels, seems to be a prime factor/force in the current religious conflicts?

There seems to me, that there has always been some conflict between different religions, and some conflict inside of the same religions, but not since the middle ages and the enlightenment has it been near as severe as now?

Religion has once again morphed into a cultural, nationalistic battle ground.

Where the Founding Fathers of our United States, in the near miraculous understanding that governments that do not separate church from state cannot stand, later administrations have seem to have lost that understanding?

It seems evident to me that starting with the cold war, where; on the one hand, the communists (USSR) proclaimed that they were a godless state and President Eisenhower had the Pledge of Allegiance to The Flag altered to include "Under God"; I suppose, to set up the concept that God was on the side of the United States against Communism?

This is not the first time this type of rhetorical activity has held sway in world history. I will get at this in more detail in the section I call "SPIN", later in the project, but for now, back to the ramifications of the various levels of fear in the current world situation.

I hope you, the reader, are able to bear with me on these various asides from the main subject, as they are what I think about and how my mind works.

I must assume that, how I think, is in a node to node and back and forth manner, in order to gather enough relevant data to continue on with the primary subject at hand?

Again, another aside, the whole objective of this and my prior work is self analysis, and as I write each line on each subject, more of who and what I am comes to light.

It seems that sometimes I control the flow and at other times the flow controls me?

I was going to save the last as a part of the conclusion of this work, but is seems appropriate to interject it here too?

Now: back to the main thread, FEAR.

There seems to be paranoia, bordering on the manic, within the two major religions of today, Islam and Christianity, such that the very cultural fibers of the respective communities are at risk?

We are for all practical purposes, in a holy war!

My last question, before leaving the religious portion of this section: are the various religious groups, from their point of view, worrying about the end of days, or are they so tired of carrying the burdens of life that they are trying to bring them about?

Now: on to FEAR, as a political tool.

I think it is a two edged sword, on the one hand each politician, whether secular or spiritual, is afraid of loosing his or her position of power, and uses fear as a means of manipulating the collective politic to maintain that position?

I operate on the premise (think), that diplomacy and ultimately war are the direct result of a very sad mix of any or all of the above.

Enough said!

Free Will

I have and will again use the term free will.

This section will make clear, or as clear as my thinking process allows, my definition of free will.

It seems to me that there are several layers or levels that take part in the free will process.

I am sure that they were laid down as part of the evolutionary process, both genetically and culturally, and because of this operating premise, I will start by analyzing "R"; or the old brain, the reptilian brain?

Maybe the first decision process was fight or flight; we made a choice to run or stand our ground.

We exercised our will to make what ever decision we made.

I am operating on the premise that as the species evolved from the invertebrate to the vertebrate, aquatic to land, reptile to mammal, to primate, there were habit patterns laid down that became instinctual or more or less hard wired though genetic natural selection and early cultural foundations.

Along with the above process we learned what to eat & drink that wouldn't kill us. In each case an exercise of will.

Somewhere along the line, "Altruism" became a third choice, run, fight, eat or not, share with and protect you close kin, in order that they my do the same for you later, and increase the potential for reproducing more kin in the future?

Of course I don't know the details of this multimillion/billion year process of evolutional and cultural development; so I must use some of the data, information, knowledge and specific results that have been compiled over the years.

In the area of social creature cultures, of which we are one, the pheromone, a scent bearing set of molecules are available and used for recognition and other aspects of community life i.e., the scent line laid down by the foraging ant, to the rest of the nest where a new food source is located or the rutting stag and/or the menstruating female of many species that entice sexual activity to propagate the various species.

Relatively recently our scientific community has uncovered at least one specific usage of pheromones in our specie.

It seems that our bodies produce a pheromone that when sensed by another of the opposite sex, can through whatever evolutionary directed, unconscious process, tell that the other party is far enough separated, genetically, that they could produce viable offspring.

It follows that if this is the case; and enough empirical evidence has been compiled by competent biologists for them to purpose it as a fact of nature and life, if an individual can isolate non-kin through the process of analyzing the pheromones, they can also isolate kin and even the level of kinship?

The above was all about the rise of altruism, that facet of the animal kingdom, us included, seem naturally to take care of their own, in most cases, most of the time, under most circumstances, in order too, or at least enhance and/or cause the continuation of the genetic/hereditary line?

We now have three sets of subconscious and/or unconscious activities working.

What to eat, when to run, and what to protect.

The real point of all the above, in this section, is the unconscious part.

There is every reason to believe, or at least it is an operating premise of mine, to assume the 80%, procedural, and 20%, declarative, heuristic in the manner of unconscious vs conscious activity in our brain/mind?

80% of the process is done at the unconscious level and then sent along to the conscious level for final 20% processing.

In a word; the several modules of the brain that are involved in unconscious mental processing compile a scenario and send it on to the pre-frontal cortex, the module that houses our conscious functions, for final processing and action.

Neuroscientists have, through years of precise and repeatable experiments come up with the time table of how fast an impulse moves along the route from touch to awareness, for example.

From the study(s), we (they) know (surmise) that things happen in microsecond periods.

For my purposes here; I purpose that the unconscious 80% of the process that goes into making a particular decision travels from node to node in the operating system and then sends the data, along with the tentative decision to the 20% conscious area for final processing, and to be acted upon.

I purpose that there is two (at least) routes for the data packet to reach the conscious; one route takes 500 micro seconds, the other only take 250 microseconds.

The reason for the two or more routes is to make sure that the data is not lost or garbled along the way, and misunderstood.

However; this is not the final result, the first potential/action data package reaches the pre-frontal cortex and is processed, then the second (or more?) packet is received.

Before the action can be triggered, the conscious process has the opportunity to veto the unconscious impulse?

This is where free will comes in: at the conscious level there is time to reconsider the potential action; in relation to real time and real action space, that was driven by old hardwired evolutionary and cultural premises during the sub/unconscious processes.

What used to work when the original processes were laid down does not always work in the brave new world.

Therefore, we have the free will to act on or veto any given impulse.

Each decision we make will have a bearing on every decision we make in the future, so in a sense each act of free will, or decision we make, sets up constraints, habits and/or parameters for all future acts that will limit our free will.

There will be more about these limitations in a later section.

Genetic And Epigenitic

This section will be about my heredity and environment and/or nature and nurture that helped make me what I am and what I might have been under a different environmental and natal situation, and maybe some connection to the specie as a whole?

I know a little about my heredity, or linage, if you will.

The following is/may be part family urban legend, some genealogy search by a late uncle and some self generated romanticism.

When I think about things, I often plug or fill in the blanks with extrapolations that may or may not be logical and/or reasonable, (rationalities), but that seem to fit after they have filtered through my unconscious and my parochial biases, and peculate up to the conscious level.

As far as I can tell, at some point around 700 AD my ancestors moved to the North of France, around Le Harve, where through what ever situation, became part of Charlemagne's Court?

There is some evidence that they were part of the financial establishment that Charlemagne set up around 800 AD, when he became the Holy Roman Emperor?

At some point after that, in a changed political situation, my ancestors, or some in my direct line, migrated to Scotland.

From there they were moved to Northern Ireland with the Scottish migration initiated by King John to pacify the country?

From what I understand, he took a page from Micaville and replaced one population with another in order to have control?

What ever the case, from there, my Grand Father came to America in the late 19ᵗʰ century.

He married a Welch woman, and my mother was on of several children that lived.

My mother ran off with a half breed Scoth/Navaho-Apache Indian apple picker, and I was born.

The above is not meant to an auto biography, but the perceived (family urban legion) linage of my personal genetic heritage?

Now: to nature and nurture.

I was born early, in a very traumatic fashion and thrown away for dead, while the caregiver (doctor?) saved my mother from bleeding to death.

My aunt Ethel, who was there at the time, said that I put my hands on the edge of the pan I had been dropped into and looked the edge at her?

She said my little head, covered with bright red hair was crushed like a prune.

She did the best she could and tried to shape my head as round a possible.

She saved my life, as broken as I was.

The above is presented here to form a basis for what I think about when it comes to heredity and environment (nature and nurture)!

I think that I (we?) was/are the basic result of a long line of commingling hereditary strains.

At the point of the sperm meeting the egg, it is all genetics, from then on it moves from nature to nurture.

What the host mother (my mother) did, does or has done in the realm of nutrition and healthy life style, will (did) reflect on our (my) chances for a relatively normal survival.

I am aware that all of the above has been covered by many people under various circumstances, and that my particular circumstances are not unique, but some new information has come forth that may, should, will have to, change the way business is done around the world.

There has been a lot of discourse on and about Global Warming, its results and possible solutions.

The reason for this work is to analyze how and what I think about, and this section is somewhat about how my thinking process may differ from the norm.

Now back to Global Warming: I think that what we should be addressing is not our use of hydro-carbons and other aspects of pollution, but the air pollution itself and what it is doing to our species chance of survival.

Current accepted science tells us that, yes, there is a 90% probability that human intervention is abetting the current trend in Global warming and that if we could stop all usage of hydro carbons right now, it would take 30 years for the current green house gasses to dissipate.

This seems to be telling the powers that be that, sure we should do something about the situation, what's the rush.

I suggested above that it is a matter of survival, and I know that this is a big jump from bad weather and rising sea levels, but current data implies that many of the problems with our new born are epigenic, that is the toxins in the air are modifying the way genes are working in the embryonic stages, to the babies detriment.

In a word, we are breathing our selves to extinction!

From my point of view and the way I think, my operating premise is, we, the collective world society, are operating in normal mode, in that we often overlook the long term results of current issues?

Case in point, the rhetoric is all about global warming, which seems to be a fact.

The mean temperature around the world is rising and many changes are taking place in our ecosystems, in the form of melting ice caps and climate changes that are moving habitats slightly northward, and weather patterns that fall out of the norm.

What we are not addressing is that it makes no difference if Global Warming is man made, partially man made or just a cycle of nature?

We focus all our energy in the debate over how and when to reduce green house gases to stop global warming and its ramifications i.e., from the above, melting ice caps and weather changes, when we should be focusing on damage to the specie.

In a given situation or problem the area of focus usually gets most attention and the severity of that focus results in a serious and immediate response. In the case of Global Warming, the scientist tell us that even if green house gas emissions were stopped now, it would be at least 30 years before we would note a drop in temperature?

Thirty years, what's the rush?

Wrong focus!

Extinction, My God, lets do something now!

It is, or has been said that the approach we are taking toward Global Warming is fuzzy science, but more and more broken babies is not fuzzy, it is a fact, and the air quality is a prime factor, and if we, the collective society doesn't do something serious and quickly, the end of days that a portion of our global society seem to be striving for will certainly come about.

Much of the debate hinges on what any change of world policy would cost, and I, a bean counter, whose main focus is economic, have come to the conclusion that cost is irrelevant, given the real problem.

I personally, as I have said over and over again, am pragmatic, a Deist, a fatalist, and have severe and acute paranoia, and operate on the premise that, we, the collective human race are too dumb to survive and are already dead and extinct, but have not laid down yet!

It probably won't happen in my lifetime, but if the generations to follow are not given the chance to have their genetic capabilities and limitations, maximized and minimized, and their environment cleaner, it won't take long.

Perhaps, then, another species will rise to the top of the food chain, and they and their generations may find a way to get off this rock before the sun explodes and ends the solar system as we knew it.

We can live if we really want to, but we have to get our head out of the sand and do it ourselves, for there is no outside influence that going to do it for us.

Goal

Given: That the Creating Force is in the Sixth Face of God (sixth house/window); (ref: "How and Why I think as I do"; 'On God'), does the creator-the creating force, in the vernacular 'God', have a goal for creating the universe?

Given: That I (we, men, homo) seems to have a propensity toward achieving perfection, and

Given: That I (we, men, homo), am/are/were created in the image of God, can there be a correlation/regession between men and God i.e., mans goal is perfection/ Gods goal is the perfect man?

Given: That the above is correct, what is the purpose of Gods perfect man?

Given: That the very evolution of man is a Russian Doll of symbiot and host functions, could God have the goal of the perfect man as a host, as the corporal entity for the manifestation of the Creative Force, to become the very soul of this perfect man?

Given: The above as fact, what responsibility has man to God?

Answer: Man must survive in order to fulfill the goal of the creating force, through his use of free will!

Given: That the creation was/is of the intent stated above, what of the creation itself?

Conjecture: The creating force (God) set the initial conditions for the beginning of the universe(s?) via the big bang; our name for the start of our facet of the creation.

Given: That the initial conditions were set up to give a determinate, but not pre-destined result?

Question: Did the creating force need more than one universe to insure that the goal would be met?

Answer: What ever the creating force had created, only our universe is of our concern.

Conclusion: We must act as if only we can fulfill the goal of the creating force and survive as a specie, to the best of our ability, as I stated above, through our use of the free will allowed in a determinate system with constraints and parameters, but no pre-destined result.

In a word, the fate of the creating forces goal is in our hands.

Government

I touched some on the collective will in the last section, but will now look at governmental aspects in more detail.

A government for the people and by the people:

What government is and does is not always what government should be and should do?

I touched this subject in my last work, "How and Why Do I Think as I do", but only in the sense of its connection to the early civilization (City Dwelling, by definition) process i.e., a city council comprised of a leader from each neighborhood, ethnic group and/or any of the various conclaves within the cities parameter, that laid down rules governing the common areas of the city i.e., the market place and or bazaars.

The most common representation/presentation of these early organizational results is the Hammurabi Code.

I will use this system as a basis for my thoughts on modern governments, but mainly about the United States of America version of local, city, state, and federal entities, with some allusion to other general forms.

The United States of America was set up by the founding fathers as a Republic, a tightly knit organization of the collective states, each with certain sovereign rights that did not and could not override the central, Federal Governments sovereign rights.

A first premise was the separation of Church and State!

It has been said that the founding fathers acted as Deists, a religious entity, an outcome of the enlightenment that held God as a Cosmic force and the creator of the Universe, and that our motto, "In God We Trust", was a statement of belief that God had done such a good job of setting up the initial conditions leading up to the Creation, that, He, She, They, or it, did not have to every again interact with the Creation or the created.

To paraphrase, 'we trust in God that men control their own destiny, as in determinate, within the laws of nature and free will, but not pre-destined or adjusted from without'.

Another first premise was the right to tax to raise operating capital to support government functions, the first basic taxes being the tariff and corporate tax.

Note:
Let me make it clear, once again, that what I think and think about may be far afield from core reality, but the use of whatever data I have assimilated and my reaction to it after the filtering of my sub conscious and my parochial bias.

Now back to taxation:

The Founding Fathers utilized the European idea of the corporation.

The State or governing agency issued a charter to the corporation to do a certain task and set up a policy that those involved were only liable for the money they had put into the enterprise. In other words the corporation was an entity, with limited liability, in its own right.

The government then took (taxed) a percentage of the funds generated by the corporation, usually 50% after expenses.

The current tax system has passed this idea down to the individual, the non-corporate business, partnerships and fiduciary enterprises, with various tax rates on profits or income.

The basic idea of this 'Tax Code', is to spread equitably the expense of government among those who benefit from the services provided, and as an aside to redistribute the wealth downward from the more affluent areas of society to the less affluent areas?

The above, I know, is pretty nebulas, but I am sure that the reader has enough personal data to fill in the blanks to satisfy their personal need and/or understanding of this aspect of government?

More about this later in more detail, and some directed comment on whether this is working or not?

Another first principle of government is the right to go to war to protect the Republic.

Our U.S. republic is based on the democratic system organized or instigated by ancient Greece, or at least they get credit for it?

A certain group of individuals in the society have the right (privilege?) to give their opinion (vote) how the republic and each governing agency should operate.

At the onset of the American Republic, that voting right (franchise) was granted to majority (over 21 years of age) white male citizens that were land owners.

That franchise has grown over the years to cover all citizens 18 years or older.

A basic review; though I am sure it is not necessary, but in order for the proper flow of this section, of our governmental structure, as set up in the Constitution.

There would be three branches: Congressional, in two houses, one house elected by popular vote from each state, allocated by one representative per a certain number of people, and the other house, the senate, to be made up of two senators from each state, at the beginning appointed by the governor of the various states, one from each political party, to achieve balanced representation, from our then limited two party system, but later changed to election by popular vote, perhaps because some governors we not appointing diverse enough senators?

The next branch after the congressional was (is) the executive, this organization led by the president, with the aid and advice of a cabinet of leaders of various areas of government was to manage the republic, via the tenets set down by the congress, with the added responsibility of the president to be the commander and chief of all military operations and has the right to wage war, within the parameters laid down by congress?

The last, but not least branch was (is) the judicial: The Supreme Court.

The function of this court was initially to make sure that any laws passed by the congress were allowable according to the constitution.

This function also covered how these laws were interpreted and utilized my the various agencies of the executive, and the State level agencies, that were (are) a miniature copy of the Federal System?

From my point of view, and the premises that I operate from, the above covers the basic intent of the Founding Fathers?

I will now get into the meat of this section: Where is our government now, and is it working successfully or failing in any or all areas, and what can be done about the failures?

Starting at the local levels, the small cities, large cities, counties, and the State level:

Some small cities are having economic situations that their local tax bases, with their current tax rates, can't alleviate!

As this is not the case of all small cities, if a study of the ones that were working well were made, we might get a handle or at least a better handle on an economic solution for the failing small cities.

There is also crime and associated drug problems at all levels, that I will address later.

I have already touched on our aging infrastructure problem in all areas, so I won't cover it here again.

I am coming to the conclusion that that I won't have to differentiate the local agencies after all, but cover the local problems as a whole.

The method for gathering taxes and the amount of taxes gathered are not satisfactory in many areas?

The services that have become necessary to be provided by these agencies have grown exponentially, while the taxing process has grown only mathematically.

Barring rampant waste and graft, the problem or part of the problem is that our current social and cultural service needs have grown larger than the current tax rate can handle.

We, as a people, individually and collectively seem to abhor taxes, but still want the collective services they provide.

Part of the solution will have to be a change of this attitude, and a larger percent tax rate will have to be put in place, while at the same time more checks and balances must be put in place to stop waste and graft.

This brings me to the penal system and in a round about way, the school system.

We spend more money supporting each prisoner that we do on the education each of our students.

Our prisons are overflowing with relatively minor drug convicted individuals, that in some (many?) instances are still getting drugs and a free ride from society.

This is ridiculous and cannot stand!

I think we should look or take a world view of the drug problem and see if any other country (countries) or societies has a handle on the problem and if they do we should something on that order in place.

A level of decriminalizing and taxation may be one answer?

A look backwards to the time of the red light districts of the past may give us a hint of how to solve the problem?

For instance, take a look at Nevada, where many of the 'sins' that are not tolerated (?) else where in the United States, are legal there.

Other areas for 'Adult Recreation' could be set up to isolate the exercising of the various recreations and the taxing of them could be set up?

Given a situation of this nature, we would have to adjust our ethical, moral and religious attitudes about capital crimes and punishment.

Given a controlled 'Recreational' situation and the taxation connected, make it a capital crime, with the death penalty, to indulge in 'Recreational' activities outside of the allocated areas, and a capital crime, with the same penalty for evasion of the taxes connected.

I know this sounds harsh, but economic and social stability will have to be put on the front burner, it our society is to survive.

As for the current batch of petty drug related prisoners, put them to work on public projects, such fire fighting and cleaning up the forests, and preventive medical research for those on death row.

I know that this may sound extreme, but the country is spiraling downward into a debt situation that could and will, if not alleviated, drive our society to collapse.

We cannot, any longer afford to let the antisocial drain our resources at the expense of the decent citizens.

As an aside: In order to implement such new ideas into the criminal justice system, we would have to alter the way we handle the prosecution side of the law that cuts corners and flaunts proper procedures in order to convict, with severe penalties, up to and including capital punishment.

As for the world wide suppliers of drugs, we could implement international controls though taxation that could not only enhance social programs, but in some cases even discourage the suppliers because of the tax burden.

We are, in a sense, part of a biological system; as in all biological systems when a cell goes haywire you kill it or it will kill you!

The drug problem is a growing cancer on our collective body, and we must control it before it kills us.

As to the rest of the economic situations that create short falls in the basic needs of our functioning society, the collective must provide the funds to support those wants and needs?

I have, or will state else where in this work, the facts or predictions concerning the reduction in the standard of living of first world countries as the standard of living in the second and third worlds rises, due to the fixed and limited recourses available on this rock we call earth, unless the first world countries increase their research into and the use of alternate energy sources i.e., solar, wind, nuclear, hydrogen and reusable plants.

Also, if the population growth does not stop, the human race will go extinct!

The only force that can stop this growth is the force of government or governments i.e., a revamped U.N.?

After the above minor tirade, I will now get back to the federal level of government economics.

The congress has the power to legislate any necessary laws that are needed for the balance of economic situations.

In order to do this, they (we) must first open our eyes to the reality that their job is not to keep their job, but to do their job and serve the people.

The entire system must be reformed so that the public and not narrow special interests are served.

This will not be easy!

As it stands now, a highly qualified pool of individuals cannot be elected to a nation office, due to the financing structure of the election process, and this has got to be changed.

In an unbiased system of hiring bureaucrats, of appointing personal to positions of power and influence, there is a ridged set of attributes, or there should be, that must be in place for an individual concerned to be given the post.

A similar system could be for potential political candidates.

If the candidate does not have the proper qualifications, then he/she cannot run for the office.

A look at history at the peak of the ancient Chinese civilization, one of the most efficient in the history of man, will show that they operated on such a system.

Children from all levels of society we tested, and if they excelled they were sent for training for the bureaucracy, and during that training the psychopaths and anti-social were weeded out.

In other words, they were trained to serve the public.

We might take a look at something like that.

Once again I stress that I understand that these ideas border on severe, in respect to our idea of how a democratic republic should be conducting itself?

However; to me, it seems evident that the principles now operating in government circles i.e., graft, lobby scandals, pork, sex scandals, church influences outside the areas of morals and ethics, and all the other various special interest bias, that are really not benefiting the overall goals of a democratic republic?

I have wandered for afield from my primary purpose of what I think about to the above ideas of how we might change it.

My main thrust here is to try to make the point that like many social, political systems of the past, many of which failed, our political system does not seem to operate as it should for the maximum benefit of the people or the state!

If this is true, we should remember all the great empires of the past that declined and fell.

I am afraid that it we don't take a good look at ourselves, and make some changes; we will follow the same path.

There is already some obvious decline!

Hospitals

When I was very young, I often heard that hospitals were where you went to die.

More recently it is the rest home or the hospice where you go to await death.

But also, many people do die in the hospital, for other reasons than they went in for!

In the vernacular, 'hospital death' is the term for this situation.

As is usual with 'vernacular', it is associated with something that is very common and excepted, and/or expected.

I don't think it should be the case with 'hospital death'.

I hear or have heard lots of lip service for the causes for this phenomena i.e., MSRA, lack of standard procedures (alluded to in another section), mistakes, errors, accidents, and other unforeseen incidents.

I think this is inexcusable and must be remedied.

While great strides have been made in medical treatment and care, people are still dying needlessly, why?

I will first look at the reasonable side of the question.

Our population is growing older, due to improved medical breakthroughs, so there are more people going through the hospital process, so as the number of deaths unrelated to the initial purpose of the visit may be increasing, we should make sure it is not just the actual number, but the percentage per 1000 or 100,000 to make sure we have correlation with regression?

With the globalization process, more and more new diseases are showing up in the hospitals that have never been seen in the United States before.

This can cause miss diagnosis, if the symptoms are similar to a know disease.

As our medical skills continue to improve we are trying procedures that would not have been attempted in the past, and the lives lost in the process may be less than it would have in the past, had they not attempted the new procedures, thus adding to the death count, while actually saving lives?

And perhaps most important, bacteria and viruses are becoming immune to many antibiotics.

The other side of the coin is what I will call the rationalization syndrome, where economics, greed, carelessness, apathy, and various 'administrative issues' are all a part of the problem.

While there are a large number of fine and dedicated institutions and staffs in the medical industry, it has still evolved into and industry and comes in under the 'capitalist' umbrella.

For the most part, hospitals, HPO, and the more recent addition, the clinic, are profit bases organizations.

It is often in the news media that some of these types of operations are being sued, alone with their insurance carriers for dragging their feet during the approval of service phase of hospitalization and treatment.

Another factor, or so it seems, the instances of the drugs not being what they were supposed to be, by being watered down or diluted, and even sub standard manufacturing policies outside the pharmaceutical industry and guidelines?

This combined with under and over medication and over billing medi-care and medic-aid adds to the problem.

With the addition of the above, as alluded to in another section, some, maybe many hospitals are outdated, poorly funded, poorly administrated and running in the red, therefore leading to a decrease in the value of the service and leading to more deaths.

When I started this project, and my other work, it was only to be a self analysis to find out who and what I was and how I thought and why, but it has grown, more or less, pulled by its own boot straps to an analysis and critique and even a harsh view of the entire societies and/or cultures of the world.

It was not my intent, but I have come to the realization that I am uncomfortable with many of the human traits that I am starting to be aware of through my self analysis process of what I think about.

Although, I operate on the premise that most individuals, most of the time, under most situations, act decently, more and more individuals, groups, cultures and even entire national governments are not decent, by the definition of what values I was brought up with in this country?

The above is, I know, far removed from hospitals, but it became part of the thought flow at this point and is too important to overlook here or anywhere else.

Injustice

There are many real and perceived injustices, but I am only going to cover that part connected with the criminal justice system.

I will start with a paraphrased newspaper headline often seen in the past few years.

'Investigations find that several of the states death row inmates have been proven to be innocent of the crimes they were accused.'

'Forensic specialist found to have been falsifying evidence results to insure that prosecutors got convictions'.

'Death row inmate proved innocent when it was discovered that the main witness against his was the actual guilty party'.

'Our county jails and state and federal prisons are filled to the bursting point with minor drug related inmates'.

'Defense lawyer sued for not properly defending client in criminal case has been found liable'.

'Prosecuting attorneys and police officers found guilty of falsifying evidence and committing perjury to get convictions.'

And one more, no so common since 'Miranda': Accused not given the opportunity to have legal council during interrogation.

And last, but by not means least, prime suspect in the crime released and set free on a technicality.

And as an aside: snitches being allowed to walk for crimes, in order to get a bigger fish.

Another aside, the police woman acting as a hooker to entrap would be johns.

There are many more, but this will get the point across that there needs to be some changes in the criminal justice system.

In the order of the above presentations, I will address each issue with I am sure, some of the overlap and redundancy that is found in most of my tirades.

Many murder trails and/or death row trials are finalized or won by the prosecution due to eye witness testimony.

It has been shown over and over again that eye witnesses are mistaken at least as often as they are right and worst yet, wrong as much a 80% of the time.

This is seen many times when the accused is a minority, because to paraphrase and old adage: 'They all look alike to me'.

Furthermore; there have been many highly acclaimed academic studies that have proven given an incident with several 'eye witnesses', there is absolutely no consensus on who or what the guilty party was wearing.

And even overriding this, when a defendant has corroborating testimony that he/she was elsewhere at the time of the incident, the jury still convicted due to eye witness testimony, maybe because they can't admit to themselves that eye witness testimony is shaky, to say the least, or last but not least, the police wouldn't have arrested the person if they weren't guilty.

As to the above, many of the actual perpetrators of the crime have been found guilty through DNA evidence or even just a review of the case files by an outside, objective, trained observer.

As to the forensic misconduct, something is being done in this area. In enlightened jurisdictions, the CSI departments are at arms length from other police activities.

Although they do cooperate, the CSI people, in the best case, are well trained and objective observers that are not directed toward a conviction, but only the truth.

In the case of witnesses giving false testimony, some prosecutors don't investigate the witness, but just use their testimony to get a conviction.

As to this and other weaknesses in the prosecuting area, there doesn't seem to be any followed guidelines, actively pursued, in place, to prosecute these offences.

The next issue, the over crowding of prison facilities with minor drug offenders is an example of laws being passed, more or less in panic, to stem the tide of certain anti-social act that the law makers think can be regulated with the threat of incarceration. Wrong!

An anecdotal connection here; it has been documented and commented that the drug related prisoners still get drugs in jail, and we also pay their room and board!

Incarcerating petty small time dealers and users is not the answer; we must get a handle on the demand issue, and then the supply.

While I was employed as a systems analyst before retirement, when ever I uncovered a problem, it was also my responsibility to supply a solution or an alternate solution.

In some societies, world wide, while there is this same drug problem, it is not in all societies?

What are those societies without overflowing drug related jails doing?

Look also on the supply side; the real issue here is that it is a large money making operation, often supported by local or state governments, or at least out of their control.

If we can't or won't do what's necessary to stop the supply side, we must do more on the demand side.

My thought is to make it legal and then tax it out of existence, with the penalty for this type of tax evasion a capital crime.

I know that this is harsh, but if at some point the economic impacts of these activities are not stopped, they will bankrupt the country.

A next issue, not yet addressed, but covered in the blanket paraphrase: 'our country has the best legal system in the world, if you have the money to buy it'.

Guilty or innocent, it seems that the rich are found innocent more often than the poor.

This problem goes hand in hand with the falsifying of evidence that the poor cannot afford to investigate and refute.

Some of our ideas in law and order must be revisited and reformed.

The idea that the state wouldn't have you on trial unless you were guilty is too prevalent in the eyes of many jurors.

I guess it all goes back to a good defense!

Next: the other side of the coin; the guilty being released due to some technical error in the police/prosecution case.

Although I understand the basic premise of English law, that ten guilty should go unpunished lest one innocent man be convicted, is not working in this case.

And last but not least; the sting, the petty criminal being let go to get the higher up, or the police woman posing as a hooker to trap Johns and stop prostitution?

Get real people, this sort of thing does not work, in the long run.

I have a plan, thought cold and without mercy, would stop all this.

When you are born, you get a thousand points and when you use them up you die.

End of Story!

Reason for the above: it all boils down to economics; when will we realize that as a nation and a race, our very survival is dependent on maximizing the use of our resources.

Ka Ma Ka Ze (The Devine Wind)

Kamakaze: the suicide pilots from Japan during World War II.

Suicide bombers: their equivalent in our current conflict with extreme fundamental Islam.

Near the end of World War II, the pilots were chained in.

I have heard the some suicide car bombers were duct taped to their steering wheels. Was it to keep them in the car, or was it another trigger to blow up the car if the driver was tried to be taken from the car after being stopped before the bomb was detonated?

We probably don't want to take this as a sign that the insurgents are running out of suicide bombers.

It doesn't seem to be the case, so we shouldn't think that there is a lessening of the enthusiasm for this type of activity either by the planners or participants.

If there is a chance that the zeal to meet Allah, as a martyr, is waning, or that the planners attitude on how to conduct this war is changing, we should take advantage of the situation as much a possible.

The Kamakaze attitude is not limited to the enemy!

Some of our military/diplomatic ideas/plans are also suicidal.

The unwillingness of the current administration to have one on one talks with 'rouge' States is not working.

Our sanction policies are only bringing more hate, resentment and resolve on the part of the States involved, to say nothing of what it does to the man on the street, in the involved States.

The idea of treating Governments or States, or States within States like naughty children has got to stop, mainly because of the energy that it drains off from other 'diplomatic' solutions, and the fact that it doesn't work with the extreme radical organizations or their satellites.

The radical organizations have not been looked at clearly by the US or the UN.

The Liberal Democratic States that are working or have worked in the past as stabilizing forces in their respective areas all have been vary closely associated with the attitudes that came out of the enlightenment period of the 17th & 18TH centuries, and were associated with Christian, Catholic and or Jewish states only.

If you have a socialist/communistic oriented populous and overlay democratic ideas to the political process, you select a socialist/communistic government with the vote, but you don't turn the state into a liberal democracy, but a legitimate Socialist/Communistic State.

The same goes for states that are infused with fundamental Islamic ideas, the elected governments are still fundamental Islamic organizations and their attitude toward western democracy and ideas and positions on the global scene go unchanged.

The 'Devine Wind' policies of all parties involved have driven us, the world as a whole, into an all out religious war!

While the current US Administration, being heavily influenced by the extreme right wing Christian, and the world wide trend toward extreme fundamental Islam, the unrest and poverty in 2nd an 3rd world countries, combined with the mass migration of poor Muslims to first world countries is a combination that has the potential for world wide terrorist activities.

I don't have the answers to these problems, but the collective United States voter in mid-term elections of 2006 voted their opinion and broke the choke hold that the current right wing Christian driven administration had on Congress.

I am not anti Christian/Islam, even though I am a Deist; however, the extreme branches of the religious right Christian and the fundamentalist Islam factions are very active participants in the current world situation.

One small case in point is the fiasco in Afghanistan, where recently Christian Missionaries were trying to convert Muslims cause an international incident.

The founding fathers of the United States established the longest existing Liberal Democratic State on the basis of absolute separation of Church and State.

This policy is, or has broken down in the United States, and was never implemented in most of the rest of the world, and I believe this has led us to the current global conflicts that are leading to the road to destroying any chance of World Peace, or for any peace, for that matter.

We all have to face up to it, if the existing cultures of the world cannot live together, they must live apart, or all die!

A solution may be for the United States and The United Nations to butt out of other peoples business, and take a page out of Teddy Roosevelt's play books and walk softly and carry a big stick?

In plainer terms, we are stepping away from your internal conflict, but if we are threatened or harmed, we will send you back to the stone age and isolate you from the rest of the world until you perish and are no longer in the gene pool!

Point: If you continue to ride the 'Devine Wind', you will end up annihilated.

This is tough love, but when you are dealing with extreme groups, the only way to overcome and restore stability is by extreme measures.

This can only work if all parties involved really understand the pending results of the current world wide activities.

Instead of a few extreme groups or States being blown back to the Stone Age, the whole world will be, and this could lead to the very extinction of the human race.

It is a forgone conclusion that if we don't get off this rock before the sun novas we are dead anyway.

Let's give ourselves a break and try to further whatever goal the Creating Force had in mind.

There will be more on the last statement, later in the work.

Language

I associate language with the spoken word, but I think (I operate on the premise that) it should also cover the written word, both written and read, and what portion of one persons intent is comprehended by the receiver or receivers.

Another facet that is important to me is semantic closure. Does the word or concept being spoken and/or written mean the same thing to all parties concerned?

It is known that there is a lack of semantic closure between and across different disciplines i.e., the various scientific fields.

It is also noticeable in mathematical notation: some different usage in, mathematics, physics, geometry and many graphical presentations are glaring.

When the above is complicating the personal data base and parochial bias of the receiver, it is a wonder that we communicate at all.

Many of the worlds' problems can be traced to misunderstandings between people, societies and cultures.

I have heard all my life that you hear what you want to hear and what you see is what you get; meaning, I think, that you hear and read what you expect to hear or read.

It has often happened to me, that when a person is relating something and the subject somewhat coincides with my preconceived cogitative flow, I stop listening to the others parties actual words and substitute my version and present it to my conscious mind.

It is said that the evolution of language is what separates Human Beings from the rest of the animal kingdom.

Does that mean that when we are acting like lesser animals that we are not using the language properly?

I think it does!

Maybe a solution too many of the world wide problems could be solved if we tried to communicate better?

Not just with lip service, but with non-political, diplomatic and/ or economic interests not overriding the need to really solve and eliminate the differences in understanding that are the basis of most problems.

Lorenz Transformation

A Lorenz Transformation is a mathematical/algebra/physics formula that describes how energy transforms into matter and visa versa.

Anyway that is my interpretation, right or wrong?

This section is not about Cosmic Phenomena, but about how things are alike.

As I go along, I will try to make the above observation a rule, fact or idea that I can depend on to help me answer the various questions that come up in every day life.

Many (most?) things can be modeled in a simpler manner than the complex reality of them, in order to understand the flows of activity in their systematic durations.

It turns out, from my perspective at least, that many models can be overlaid over many different systems with very little adjustment or change.

In the vernacular, this phenomenon is addressed as matter of scale or fractulization.

There is a partnership between Systems and models of systems.

In other sections, I will or will have covered the make up of systems in much detail, but for my purposes here, I will just say that systems have input, processing and output, not necessarily in that order (more about this part later).

Models are made the same way:

The input, usually singular or simple is described, then the process or processes are explained, then the output or outputs are defined.

This is the first level of many/most things are alike, they can mostly be modeled with the same interchangeable parts.

The next level then is a matter of scale, larger and larger systems made up of smaller and smaller systems.

The bottom line at this level is that all matter is made up of this transformation of the relatively few sub atomic energy particles and the natural laws that they operated under.

The next level; the fractal stage, is usually described as linier or outside measurements and/or shapes.

Examples are usually maps, shown from various stages of magnification of the shore line or exterior boundary of some entity.

I use the term linier here is the sense of distance from one point to another, in a straight line.

If you look at a map of the east coast of the United States the distance from the tip of Florida to the top of Maine, in a straight line is approximately 1500 miles.

If you go through the magnifying process or even just walk along the coast, you will soon see that the actual distance alone the water line, at a static tide, is far greater than 1500 miles.

There are mathematical formulas than can and have been to find these actual distances.

These mathematical formulas work with a high degree of accuracy.

I will not go into the actual formulas themselves, but try to make the point that they are just models at work.

The only way that this could be so is that there is a universal sameness in natural phenomena.

It is my operating premise, in this area, that as natural laws can be understood and modeled with some accuracy, then man made laws, traditions, cultures, language and the multiple other activities of every day life can be modeled also, with an overlay of the simple model i.e., input, process and output.

I am not overlooking the fact that as systems become more complex and self organizing due to the result of emerging processes in the gestalt mode i.e., the sum is greater then the parts, but trying to emphasize the point that steps of the process are the discrete steps followed the simple model in relative order.

At any given node in the process there are one or more steps that can and will be taken to get to the next discrete point, and that these steps are derived from the output of the previous step, liken to the simple model to the complex model i.e., one simple model piggybacked onto the next simple model.

There is no predestined result going on here, but the methodology is determinate in that there are the parameters of the natural laws; there is wiggle room, or the operating of some sort of free will operating at every step.

The point here is that at the very beginning of this subject I stated that many/most things are alike, not that all things are alike.

An example; Classical Physics was based on the premise that if you knew the initial conditions of a situation or system, you could absolutely predict the future of that situation.

As scientific knowledge grew it was found that the classical system did not work at the level of the very small.

In a word, macro systems are mostly subject to modeling in a linier manner – if P then Q.

Micro systems on the other hand, are only able to be modeled thru a system of statistical probability of this or that happening at a given time or place.

The statistical probability scenario can still be modeled as long as one understands that the result will only be determinate and not predestined.

I know that this section has wandered far afield from the starting premise, but not so far that (I at least) have lost sight of the fact that you can plan ahead (model the future), with some accuracy if you weigh all the inputs and process to the best of your ability, using the relevant data.

All other things being equal; things, are sometimes also equal?

The circle, the cycle, or what ever you wish, the bottom line is that grass grows, makes seeds, dies, and the seeds make grass, and the cycle starts all over again, understanding that neither the grass or the seeds are free from evolution.

Good modeling has the same restriction; although most/many things are alike and can be modeled, even the models must evolve to keep up with the evolution of the system being modeled, understanding that change and evolution are alike.

Motivation

This section will cover psysic/cognative motivation and not the physical movement of object or beings, which will probably be covered in other several sections.

A synonym for motivation is drive, a term used concerning movement or travel i.e., drive your car, buggy, bicycle or golf ball, or last but not least to drive someone else or even yourself crazy.

The use of the same term to define more than one attribute of the human condition is not uncommon.

One of the main reasons I stress semantic closure as one of my goals in self understanding, and also across disciplines, is this phenomena.

The ability to use terms interchangeably in various situation and/ or contexts is possible (motivated?) due to our mental capacity of language manipulation and/or understanding based on the subject being addressed by the various cognitive processes.

The above is more or less an aside from the subject of this section, but necessary to analyze how I think and what I think about.

My motivation, if you will, for these various presentations of my mental functioning i.e., How I think and What I think, it to understand, or try to understand myself, and use this as a venue or vector towards universal understanding of other individuals, groups, societies, cultures, demes, or any other collective of the specie.

What possesses (motivates) me to do these things?

I have and overpowering instinct to live!

Maslow covered the basic components of these instincts with his pyramid – paraphrased: water, shelter, food, clothing, companionship, reproduction and finally self actualizations and transcendence.

I am going to use the various aspects in many connotations to describe my take on each one and their relationships to me, this, and other subjects of analysis in this work.

First water: to drink, to bathe in, to irrigate with, too navigate on and into another category, to fish for food.

It seems to be a basic instinct to find water and then to insure that access will always be available by what ever means necessary; economic, diplomatic or war, if all else fails.

On to shelter, the last will apply, with the addition that for whatever reason (motivation?), soon after the basic roof and hearth, the style size and physical attractiveness become a factor i.e., we must keep up with the Joneses.

Next food; in the beginning it was fruit, nuts and the various animal that was killed and eaten, directly from nature with no extra effort on our their part to aid and abet their production.

Next companionship; in the beginning the individual mate or family.

A new phase begins with some wild fox or wolf puppy is kept rather than killed for food. (Motivation?, it was cute and cuddly).

This or those puppies became companions and/or watch dogs.

This was the beginning of domestication, and along with the discovery that while one was gathering grasses and seed to eat, in those places where you gleaned the grain, new plants grew the next season in greater amounts than the original.

Low and behold: the domestication of animals and plants; the agricultural revolution has begun.

The mate and family parts addressed above take care of the reproduction phase.

As each level was reached, the same activities and/or motivations to keep the products of these levels, economic, diplomatic, and/or warfare became more important.

Now we (I) have come to the self actualization and transcendence parts.

During the other phases, we had made some distinctions between what was internal to us, and more or less in our controls, and the external (nature/natural?), that was outside of our control.

We had slowly begun to question: who am I; what am I doing here, where did I come from?

We had come to realize or at least cognize the fact that some things caused other things, our first run in with cause and effect.

With this came idea of duration – this thing or things happen in a temporal manner.

At sometime in the past, something caused the start of this.

God and/or Gods were born!

Certain types of individuals, through what ever reason (motivation) began to examine the acts of God/Gods and explain them.

They came up with ideas of how to placate those (The God/Gods) or treat with them for the betterment of themselves or their community.

Thus the interactive God was born and we have been going down hill (with some flattening along the way i.e., the enlightenment and the Deists) ever since, to where we are today in a global religious war based on what each faction deems to be the will of the interactive God.

So much for motivation!

Normal

Some connotations of 'Normal' are very different from others, in the sense that the term used across disciplines has vastly different meanings.

I am aware that I bring the lack of semantic closure across disciplines into the body of many sections of this work.

The reason or at least the rational for this is to emphasize what I think about the language and how we use it from day to day in different situations, contexts, and cognitive streams.

The unique ability for the average (normal?) person to acquire the correct (normal?) meaning of a term used in a contextual/situational flow of input/output data and understand internally the meaning of the communication and to expect and believe that the receiver will receive the same message is one of the most important aspects of the human social structure.

I operate on the premise that many of the problems between individuals, groups, societies, cultures, religions and governments is that the expected result of terminology usages are misinterpreted and misunderstood, in the same dialect of the same language, and even more misunderstood across different languages.

The normal beat of language varies, the nuance and emphasis are different, the personal space of individual people and cultures differ, the translator who listens to the output of one person in one language and translates that to input in another language to another individual or individuals may misinterpret the beat or nuance of the original output, either by accident or for what ever reason, on purpose.

It is much the same with written languages.

In a good, footnoted text, the various meaning, nuance and/or connotation is listed, something that is impossible with spoken language.

In many instances the total meaning of a statement could be perceived as one of many meanings.

Cultural context is often not considered in vocal conversion of the reading of a written conversation or thought flow.

Temporal aspects are also not always considered by one or both of the parties concerned.

Cultural aspects wax and wane and cycle through many of the same trends, but the rhythm of the cycles may not be in sync.

What a statement contains now may be different from the meaning last year or ten or twenty years ago.

The point of all of the above is that there are probably more abnormal aspects of personal communication than normal.

Each participant in a dialogue has the propensity to hear what they want to hear and avoid the rest.

An example of this has been presented before i.e., if a thought stream from the speaker matches the/a representation in the listener, often the input is overlaid by the representation of the of the hearer or receiver.

And also, in the case of a good novelist, often only 20% of the plot line needs to be written so that the reader can/may supply the remaining 80% to satisfy their need for continuity and understanding.

The whole point of this section is to stress that in cross cultural situations, the most common (normal?) situations in our internal multicultural society, or the global multiculturalism, one must be very careful that they are versed in the culture of the other party/parties.

An example or examples has/have come up recently on the world stage.

The first was when the USSR came apart at the end of the cold war.

Almost immediately age old conflicts and hatreds that had been forcefully held in check by the over powering force of the totalitarian state, burst forth in civil conflicts and ethnic cleansing episodes that took international, forceful military activities to get under control.

Next: the Iraq situation, caused by the removal of the iron hand of Sodom Hussein from the throats of the Sunni and Shiite populations.

As soon as this totalitarian thumb was lifted, the two parties reverted back to the nearly 500 year battle to control Islam.

Another point: the normal democracy that the United States (and allies?) have tried to overlay over many countries and/or cultures.

A point that they are missing, is that Liberal Democracy (the type exercised in most western first world countries), was/is the outflow of the 'Enlightenment' movement that basically states that all individuals were equal and had the right to be treated such, and on top of this, the western, first world states are all Christian and/or Judaic/Christian based.

Another point: honest elections and the vote do no insure Liberal Democracy.

If the parties that vote have a cultural bent toward and ism or a particular religion, the newly elected representatives will formulate a government reflecting that culture, with all it ramifications.

Labels do not change the underlying cultural prerogatives!

Beware of using local normal innovation and situations across global cultures.

Only knowledge of and about your adversary will set you free.

Knowledge across cultures is the only real truth.

Optimism

The Expected results of optimism have some or most of the connotations of luck i.e., preparation meeting opportunity.

Being optimistic without some effort is not commensurate with success.

The standard joke about optimism is the glass is half full rather than half empty or a person really doesn't have all the facts.

Whether or not one is optimistic or pessimistic does not change core reality.

This fact tends to emphasize the idea of some philosophers and deep thinker put forth: it's all in your head.

Post modernists seem to opt toward the point of view that things or attitudes are just mental constructs.

This brings me again, around to the thought that seems to be overriding in what I think about. Possibly the majority of the U.S. population advocate to believe in an interactive God and are optimistic that what ever happens is Gods will and has to be right and that all will end well for those who keep the faith.

One of the things that they do not comprehend is that there are other religious groups around the world that believe the same thing, but their goals are not the same.

Like it or not, the world is in a religious war that has been gathering forces for decades.

That the current administrations and/or religious communities around the world, each advocating their own political/diplomatic (diplmantic) style are, 'staying the course', because they know that God is on their side, and optimistically maintain that their policy and goals will prevail is what is fueling this conflict.

The only thing that this religious based optimism does is cost countless lives, pain and suffering, to say nothing of the economic of resources that could be put to uses to enhance mankind and their goal of survival.

Our small rock, or rocket ship, is a closed community with limited resources and recuperative processes.

The laws of conservation, the very backbone of the universal (cosmic) system will insure that the balance between energy and matter will remain constant, whether we are here or not!

The law of conservation is not an entity with intent or purpose, but a natural law that is without direction or purpose except the parameters concerned with the shift of energy to matter and back again.

Our current science tells us that the Solar System is approximately 4.5 billion years old and has used about half its life span.

Given this data, we can operate on the foregone conclusion that the Sun will Nova at the end of its life.

If all of humanity (the specie Homo sapiens) still remains on the earth they will perish in the explosion, if they haven't already gone into extinction through lack of evolving and/or adaptation to the changing conditions that will bound to happen with the changing conditions of the Sun.

In either case, this means we will go extinct, as have 99.9% of all species that have ever lived on earth.

I know that this time line seems to be irrelevant to us now, but I have the fatalistic (pessimistic?) feeling that our conflicting optimisms of God's will are hurrying the extinction process.

In fact (in my mind?), I have the idea (operate on the premise that) there is a collective feel that the 'End of Days' is inevitable and that these forces are actively trying to bring it on, because they are tired of carrying the burdens of life and want it to end.

I also know that this is crazy, but it's no less crazy for a young women with a true and pure heart strapping a homemade bomb round her pregnant belly & walking up and hugging a soldier of the other team and setting off the bomb and sending them both, along with collateral damage to the feet of their respective maker, who in the point of view of most leaders of the various faiths, believe to be the same interactive entity.

Once again in my mental, personal, internal representation of the Universe, I find myself confused.

For what ever reason, I can see both sides of these issues, but can't reconcile them to core reason.

Are these activities of both camps really acts of free will or what?

I am a fatalist with a paranoid bent, and my take on the glass is that it just is, but only in passing. More on this later?

Pessisism

Pessimism in the norm is that feeling that the glass is half empty and that Murphy's Law is always in effect i.e., if any thing can go wrong it will.

This feeling is driven by a broken psyche.

Man's nature and the life force are not pessimistic.

Despondency is not the norm, but an aberration of the norm.

My take on this is if you look for trouble you may find it, the pessimist, on the other hand know that trouble will come whether you are looking for it or not.

Is pessimism at the core of discontent or is discontent the core of pessimism?

Pessimism is hurt and self humiliation, the hair shirt and flaying of religious fanatics who see this as a method of appeasing their interactive God, in order to be accepted in heaven i.e., a personal end of days through self abuse and destructive suicide.

In the eyes of some religions this is an affront to God, the throwing away of his creation.

There is no logic or reason behind these points of view, but some rationalization that some men are gifted with a pipeline to the creative force (GOD).

But how can they, in truth operate from the two different messages from the same creative force (GOD)?

I operate on the premise that if they are not insane, that they are self promoters who want personal power and all the trimmings that come with it, without regard for who is hurt by their acts.

I call them all hypocrites, and by their very existence, prove that the creative forces(s?) are not interactive with man!

The Universe is determinate but not predestined, and this allows man the ability to have free will within certain parameters according to the natural laws, but does not give us any insight into the goal(s?) of the creative force(s?), but I am sure that pessimism and its results are not part of the final goal, if there is one?

More on this later; also.

Political Trident

I have come to the conclusion (I operate on the premise) that political trends wax and wane due to the coming together and splitting apart of just 3 basic political philosophies.

A: Expanded Manifest Destiny i.e., world dominance of the current ism in vogue.
B: Pragmatic Economics i.e., what ever works for us.
C: Religion i.e., when not separated from the state.

The standard mathematical formula for the permutations of three objects are 6 associations i.e., for the three philosophies; ABC, BCA, CAB, ACB, CBA and BAC.

In the case in question; however, there are many more ramifications.

For instance, global dominance can be looked at from at least three prospective:

1. World wide democracy
2. World wide capitalism
3. One world wide religion.

The pragmatic economic have at leas three faces:

1. Laissez faire – let the market speak.
2. Resource exploitation by 1st world countries on 2nd/3rd.
3. Nationalization of all foreign enterprises.

Last but not least, religion and the state:

1. Various social situations i.e., abortion, gay marriage, scientific research.
2. The merging of church and state sets up social conflicts.
3. The tendency of a strong religion to want dominance.

The details above are just that, details that are part of the process.

Those details are not what this section is about.

This section is trying to look for trends of/in the United States of America with the weighted results of the six permutations of the political trident at work.

Weighted in order – take ABC:

What have the results been when A&B combined their efforts with C taking a minority position.

Manifest Destiny and Pragmatic Economics:

Look at several facets of the Vietnam era.

The godless Communists are exercising their own manifest destiny and the domino theory states that our manifest destiny will stop.

Add to this to the oil reserves in the South China Sea, that the governments that controlled Indo China would have access.

C & A/B together put us into the war until the collaboration deteriorated and the will to continue was lost.

What was behind this shift of power?

It was the moral and ethical response of the people of America.

The war was wrong on these grounds, and the sacrifices being made weren't worth the outcome.

Morality and ethics are the purview of religion; the C factor joined forces with the fragmenting collision of the A/B factor and stopped the war.

We could go through the other five permutations, but I don't think that it's necessary, you, the reader can do this analysis and discover for your selves what forces our political and National trends!

Also, you should spice up your analysis of each permutation with a little gender bias, racial bias and xenophobia!

Prostitutes, Police And Preachers

There is, or has been an adage that you should/could never trust anyone whose profession begins with "P".

I don't know that this is true, but I am sure (operate on the premise) that due to human nature, it is true in some cases.

I will, from my point of view, and through my thinking process, using my very fluid operating premises, analyze each of the subjects of this section.

Starting with prostitution, in my opinion, the second oldest profession:

By definition; a trading of sexual favors for material gain.

In our society this can be a business operation (other than sex) where either a man or women trades there morals and ethics for material gain.

That is not the prostitution I am addressing here, but perhaps later?

Another form, from the point of view of some, is the marriage trade off. The man or woman, who ever the bread winner is, furnishes the material gain and the other partner furnishes the sex and others work or labor for survival.

This is also, not the type of prostitution I am addressing.

I am addressing prostitution as the business of trading sexual favors for money.

Whore, Harlot, hookers or working girls are some of the labels we have put on the female participant of this activity.

My analysis will try to cover the whys and wherefores of this phenomenon that seems to be part of the fabric of all cultures, from pre-history to tomorrow.

First, I think (operate on the premise) that there has always been a division of labor and various rewards for this labor.

This situation often has caused economic strata to form within a society.

In some instances when a woman or girl cannot find, or is not trained or otherwise not capable of a specific job, she has always been able to find a man who would pay for sexual favors.

At the present moment, in the United States of America anyway, in rare cases i.e., some parts of the state of Nevada, prostitution is illegal, but still thrives or at least takes place.

At this point we brush against the other two subject of this section, the police, who try vigorously to stop, slow down, control and/or share in the profits, are suppose to do all they can to stop this criminal activity, but don't seem to accomplish much.

Then on to the preachers, who mostly seem to voice the opinion that it is a crime, not only in the eyes of man, but also in the eyes of God.

However; down through history, and even today, some of the leaders of the church have been caught with their pants down in the house of prostitution.

I guess that the main point of my thinking here is that the sex drive is so powerful that even the best of men fall prey to it.

Men have mistresses, girl friends, call girls, occasional or routine contacts with prostitutes, and women commit adultery with friends, the mailman, the plumber, the cable guy, the golf pro and many other persons of proximity, to say nothing of the ventures of same sex activity in both genders.

Then, considering the above, perhaps we should add 'persons' to our 'P' list or change the list, to only include 'persons'.

When I started this section, my goal was to analyze the economic factor involved with the 'P' people.

As usual, I have gone astray; my pencil has produced above and beyond my expectations.

So then, I should get back to the original goal.

If prostitution and its ramifications are so prevalent, why not legalize and tax it?

This would free up the police to pursue more virulent crimes and the preachers wouldn't break their vows and become hypocrites.

But mostly, we might begin to realize that we cannot legislate morals and ethics, but only control the violent acts between parties by criminalizing them.

A solution to many social problems would be to set up areas, districts, like the old red light districts, or the now common adult business restrictions, and put all of the now social sins, prostitution, drugs, gambling and various other nefarious activities in a special part of each and every town, tax the revenues, and let those who wished to pursue these activities alone.

One of the first things this would do would be to relieve the pressure and expense of maintaining prison facilities to house sex and drug violators.

As it stands now, each community in the United States spends exponentially more money on each prisoner than they spend to educate each of their children.

As I said before, this would allow the police more time to handle real crimes against people and property, and also relieve the preachers from preaching about crimes against nature and get back to the very basic goal of community service and the golden rule.

Also, this is not a new idea; it has worked well throughout history and is working now in other place in the world.

So, I guess my original premise for this section has gone down the tubes and what we (I) end up with is my normal focus on economics and religion.

Quantum Mechanics

It often comes to mind that I don't really have a handle of the very large or very small.

I perceive that the very large things, numbers, space, the universe, although grasped in their totality, are at least stable, in the sense of classical physics, where things are seen as they are.

Small, very small things on the other hand, are said not to be that stable, but can only be viewed from the point of statistically probable events.

The smallest things that I know about are subatomic particles.

Science tells me that I can find the momentum or a particle or the location of a particle, but not both at the same time.

This is called the uncertainty principle.

From my limited point of view, this has to do with the digital and analogue aspects of nature.

From the digital side of things, they have a discrete and static state, and in that phase, the individual item in question is frozen in time and space.

This digital phase is very lumpy, like tapioca pudding or the frozen bubbles in water.

Analogue, on the other hand is continuous without a break in the flow of time and space.

The electron movement in a copper wire connected to your toaster and a wall socket, while the toaster is on, are digital, however fast they are moving, they are each still discrete entities, while the gear driven old wrist watches are analogue, and their movement is continuous as long as there is an energy source, such as a wound spring.

The quantum mechanics come into play at this point, from my perspective.

A Quantum of energy is the movement of a discrete particle or group of particles, moving from one discrete static place to the next, some what like the ticking of the watch mentioned above.

Frozen in time the tick and the quantum are digital.

As long as there is enough tension on the watch spring, the watch will remain in an analogue state, but when the spring unwinds and/ or looses its tension and can no longer send energy to the gears, it will stop and once again become digital, in the sense that the parts, in their macro state, the classical state of big things, will become discrete in time and space.

They will pause in this state until I rewind my watch.

The same process is applied in my digital watch, as long as the battery is not dead; the watch will run, keep time, with a readout either digital, a LED screen, or analogue, with the hands moving around the dial of a numbered face plate.

The main reason I think about this subject is to get or try to get a handle or a better handle on the workings of nature.

I see these phenomena as matters of scale, associated with the fractal aspect of looking at things with increasingly stronger microscopes.

The more powerful the microscope, the finer the detail, until the electronic microscope that lets me view activity at the atomic level, the very heart of the quanta operation.

I don't know that I see those things as scientists do, but I see a connection between the very big and the very small as the way to broaden insight in not only what I think about, but back to how do I think in the first place.

What is the makeup of those 'emerging process' that allow the change from inorganic to organic?

What complex micro/macro mix changes the nonliving to the living?

This is really what I think about most!

All the rest of it is just a methodology I use to get there.

Quantum mechanics is as small as I can form an internal representation of; so, I have to begin there.

The reason (rational?) for this section is to try to establish data points, discrete and static, that I can weave into an analogue understanding of why and how I exist.

I must make this point, again and again.

It's all about me and the creating force(s) and the connection, if any!

Reason And Rationality

This is a return to the previous work, but expanded.

In the original "How and why do I think as I do", I discovered how and why I reason and rationalize, while in this section I will pursue what I reason and rationalize about, in the micro only, there is not enough time or space to enter the macro world of my thinking process.

When I face a mathematical or scientific situation I try to use reason i.e., gather all the data points available and follow them to their logical and exact, process end.

I try, or tell my self that I try, to be reasonable at all times, but I never, or I try to never, forget that there is no truth in logic if your basic premise is false or the result is open to interpretation.

The simple 'if P then Q' works in simple situations i.e., If it's raining, the ground is wet, unless it's covered with something to keep the water off or out.

Another 'if P then Q' that doesn't work is if the basic premise is biased or prejudiced i.e., All men are not created equal; therefore, some men should rule others for their own good. This is the elitist rational.

The above rationale is one of the basis for conflict in politics, diplomacy, economic, governmental action and most of all in religion settings.

If P then not Q, you're with me or against me, cover most of the rationale scenarios.

In economics or business; however, another or other rationales come up.

An old one was, in paraphrase, 'what's good for the corporation is good for America'.

Another was, 'our investors depend on their dividends, and if they don't get them, they will sell their stock, the price will drop, the corporate value will decline, so we must not let this happen'. In order to keep the bottom line healthy, we must cut costs.

Below are a few instances concerning the above:

The railroads cutting maintenance expenses, letting the infrastructure decline to the point that the industry all but went out of existence by loosing their market share due to accidents, increases in insurance expense, and delays causing unstable delivery of goods.

Manufacturing and/or refining plants modifying maintenance schedules or changing process without proper testing, or just cutting cost by shrinking the work force have caused many unnecessary disasters.

Look at those companies taking advantage of badly written tax laws to move their company headquarters too offshore locations to avoid paying the proper tax.

And, perhaps the most overused rationale of all i.e., its our duty to the stock holders to make a profit, case in point the railroads from above & the HMO's that refuse all claims the first time around, for various reasons, and the medical institutions that over bill medicare claims.

I could go on for several pages describing the methods that certain levels of management commit to bolster their bonus, some times to the extent that the company collapses.

The above rationales are sadly a reflection of human nature and greed that in my view, is on the rise, whether it is just due to the increase in population or the degree of morality/ethics decline.

I feel strongly and think about the following a lot, you may even say it is an obsession!

The religious institutions; which, it seems to me, should be the main source of our moral and ethical codes, have watered their message, because they are spending all of their available energy on promoting their version of the one and only interactive God.

If you sense a iconoclastic point of view here, you are right.

Many groups, communities, societies, governments, governments within governments, are being consumed with motive that are more related to their support of their various interactive gods, than to the people they are supposed to serve.

This is not the first or last time I have or will allude to the possibility that some factions of the various religious communities are striving for 'end of days', too, in my opinion, lay down the burdens and go to the feet of their personal interactive God.

I think that they may get the job done if the other parts of society don't give voice to reason, and stop them!

Recognition

From the beginning of written history, recognition has been equated with the prime drive of the species.

The subject of this section will be an analysis, from the point of view of what I think and think about on the subject of recognition.

Look at me, look at me!

What do you want? I will do any thing to please.

You have a choice; you can recognize and worship the new God or die.

We will fight, and the loser will recognize the winner as master, and the loser as slave, or we will fight to the death, then the winner will have to enter a another battle or battles until the loser is not willing to die and will become slave and recognize the winner as master.

This is a philosophical version of the need to be recognized.

I will start my view synopsis from a different facet of human nature, selfishness.

It is mine, leave it along!

I want it, let me have it!

I will hit you if you touch it!

You wanna fight?

Yea! If I win can I have it?

No never, I'll tell my mother!

Sissy! I'll tell every body you're a momma's baby.

Oh yea!

You hit me! WA, WA, I'm going home!

It may not have happened to you in that exact manner, but I am sure you understand the little back yard play about two children.

My point; perhaps, is not that we (I) may not only need personal recognition, but our (my) property and achievement are ours (mine), and must be recognized as such.

This also goes for beliefs, country, wife, family and all else that we (I) cherish, and often that overlaps into another persons perceived property.

Property, resources, economics, and self esteem all wrapped up in one ugly package; that seems to me to be the root of all evil, if not balanced and/or handled properly.

I have heard that the last resort of the down trodden is Honor, and that the hallmark of a gentlemen is his defense of his Honor, or a countries Honor and Glory are worth fighting a war over.

Maybe this section should be titled, Honor vs Recognition?

Two points here, semantics and demes.

Given a group of people, not necessarily connected by community, which is grouped together because they think and act alike in the same situation.

Semantic closure is the absolute and perfect understanding of terms and concepts across disciplines, and deme closure is in the image of a group of clones.

The two statements above are just background for entry into the complex issues raised by the complex issues raised by the various aspects of recognition and/or Honor.

Each individual, groups of like thinking individuals, or ism's (Demes), if you will, have different criteria for the recognition and/or the defense of the Honor of the organization.

The seemingly prime need, or human nature of the species, either alone, or in groups is to propagate their particular set of mores.

This is the meat of this section, until we all understand and recognize the values and mores of others there will be wars and rumors of wars.

I am not advocating a paraphrased Post-Modern idea that every individual, culture and/or society cannot be held responsible according to our mores, when he, she, or they are acting according to theirs.

My avocation, if I have one, is that in order for the species to survive in the Global Community that we find ourselves in, there must be a new recognition criteria.

We, the collective human race, must recognize that our very existence depends on a dialectic of many facets that will allow us to live in peace and prosper.

Harp, Harp, here I go again, into my main theme, if you can't insert it here, you may as well stop reading, you are not going to get my point that the avocation of multiple or singular interactive God's is not the answer to the survival to our species!

Soul

I have/will broach my concept of leakage between the Creative/Creating Force(s) and the creation in the future section on 'TRUTH'.

Given that the concept has merit, the concept of the Soul is such a leakage.

Although I am a Deist, I do not hold out that there will not be a review or judgment at the end of days or this creation.

I operate on the premise that my input will be presented to the Creative/Creating Force(s) then, for what ever it's worth.

My take on the Soul is that it, as a representation of the individual, will be the object of review or judgment.

I am well aware that the very idea or concept of the soul is a mental method of the ego to be eternal and never die.

I also feel that the ego is an emerging property of the life force that allows our existence in the first place; therefore, I value the ego idea of eternal life, at least up to the time of review and/or judgment.

My concept of the soul, as a mental representation, is something like a big 1000 mg. vitamin E pill, with the property of being able to expand and become our aura, another leakage that stores all our data, thoughts, actions, and will be available for the review and/or judgment.

This should tie into the previous subject on 'GOAL'.

Spin

Many pursuits have been given the label of the first profession, but I operate on the premise that spin may have been the very first.

Allusions to 'rhetoric'; the ability to overcome reason with rationality, has been a prevalent subject in world literature since the very onset of the written word.

Our recent pundits or talking heads have coined the phrase 'spin doctor', as if the phenomena was new to our generation, but I operate on the premise that it has been a human trait ever since the 'giant leap', that historical period when primate evolution branched into the homo species.

As I have stated before, maybe more often than necessary, even thought each of the sections of this work are able to or meant to be able to stand alone, there will be overlap, redundancy or even contradiction, due to subject, situation and complexity of subject.

After all that, back to spin.

Children may begin to use it at a very young age, when asked, 'why did your do that?', they say, often teary eyes, 'I don't know'.

The next level may be the little white lie, and then on to the out right lie, to avoid punishment.

Perhaps the next level is when parents modify the truth about various subjects when questioned by their children.

What ever the case, it seems to me to be or to have an overriding aspect/effect on/of the mental process.

Even puppies do it when caught wetting the floor.

I guess my point here is that I have to be very careful that I do not try to fool myself or others with rationale, when it goes against reason.

Although my primary goal is to produce more than I consume, prior to that is the need, or at least cognitive goal to be true to myself.

Much of the iconoclastic joust with the variances of social and/or belief systems is my trying to portray in these sections my true feeling and/or thoughts.

Once again, warts and all, what you see is what your get, after all, it's all about me, right?

What Makes The
Teletype Work

This section will try to relate some of the various connections, if they actually exist, between man and machine, and man and himself.

The man in question: me; of course!

This section may be considered as an extension of the modeling theme, alluded to before.

The focus here is on communication from one human to another via a third intermediary.

An author: his book; and the reader.

A teacher: his subject; and his student.

But; in this case, the middle entity will be a machine or machines in conjunction with one another as the intermediary.

The teletype, how does it work?

Is the teletype a model for the hearing part of the human communication system?

Up to a point it is like a radio receiver, but instead of electronic waves being transformed into sound waves as they pass through an amplifier to the listeners' eardrums, that are transformed into chemical/electrical impulses that are transmitted to various parts of the brain via more chemical/electrical venues filtered through a language module and on to the pre-frontal cortex, via a multitude of unconscious systems, decoded, then reaching awareness as music or words that one has or has not heard before, often resulting in multiple shifts of emotional shifts in the listener; they (the radio waves) enter or are received by an antenna tuned to the frequency of the teletype transmitter.

The radio waves that are already electric-magnetic waves or energy are transformed into electric current that passes through to various electrical components called solenoids that are connected to the various parts of the typewriter that the converted energy, now in variable pulse formats, that activate the moving parts of the teletype i.e., the letter keys, the carriage return and the gear that turns the roller to insure that typed letters do not overlap each other.

At this point the teletype starts typing and the noise from it attracts the attention of the receiving operator, who then goes through various scenarios to remove the message, route it to the proper party and prepare what ever response is necessary back to the originator.

The point of the above is not to give the reader a primer on the hearing process or of how the teletype works, but to add to my self analysis of what I think about and why.

I hope that I don't run you off with the reiteration that this is all about me, and if you, the reader have fought through this far, you may also have gotten some insight into why and what I think about, and maybe about yourself also?

I don't know what good it will do you to understand some of my inner workings, but the good it has done me has no bounds.

This minor pass at the interaction and correlation of men/man and machine is relevant, but not the primary function of this section.

A continuation from previous sections that have implied that things are alike; is the motive here.

If I can discover the various simple models that the natural laws provide, perhaps I can use them to eliminate the unnatural facets of my thinking process and get closer to becoming one with the universe, and through that process, become one with myself and others.

Travel

Travel broadens ones outlook is a thought that seems to be prevalent in most societies, but when you come across aspects of the new places that have customs or traditions alien or even abhorrent, do you broaden or shrink?

In early societies, most people, most of the time, lived and died a short distance from where they were born, even the hunter/gatherer/nomads had a relativity fixed area of occupation.

Today most people, most of the time, live for a while, at least, hundreds or even thousands of miles from where they were born.

In some cases, maybe due to globalization and downsizing, some people are moving back to the parents' home that may or may not have been where they were born.

Since the earliest societies, some people were travelers, adventurers, traders or just migrated singularly or in mass.

I guess my point here is that travel and people movement seems to be a part of human nature that is expanding.

Economics has something to do with it, as the move from the farm to the city, or in the current situation, people following jobs to new places, either across borders or over seas.

Our traveling and moving about the world; however, is overtaking our evolution.

Although man is the only animal able to live almost everywhere on earth, many times the movement has been into areas where the person's immune system cannot compete with the local pathogens.

Worse yet, infections that rise in one part of the world can be and have been transported by plane and ships to the rest of the world, to say nothing of what some flora and fauna have done and are still doing to the ecosystems and economics of their transplanted homes.

I don't want to say that we, as a specie, are short sighted or paint this situation with too broad a brush, but I will say we are slow learners when it comes to fouling our own nests.

This phenomena can be or has been caused by 'well; I just didn't know this would happed' to 'it's not my problem' to 'it's got to be fixed by so and so', and maybe most of all 'it would cost too much and put us in bankruptcy'.

The crux of all of the above is that travel or its result; the movement of people and things, have not always been beneficial or broadening.

At another level, in a global society, the direction we seem to be going, a universal or collective mind set must evolve, if we, as a specie, are to continue.

The 'United Nations' ideas' have evolved to being a peace keeping and aid organization.

These ideas are being addressed after the fact!

If we are going to survive, as a viable global society, we are going to have to get ahead of the power curve, and eliminate the needs for the conflicts that demand peace keeper and aid organizations.

We must isolate the causes of the conflicts in the world and through some dialectic diplomatic process, eliminate these causes or we will destroy ourselves before the sun blows up and does it for us.

And that brings me to the real travel issue; if we don't get our act together and martial our resources, both mental and economic, and get off this rock, our specie will die here!

Truth

In philosophy, science, religion and psychology, by definition, there have been three types of truth.

Coherent truth, where all the ideas, input, output and/or conclusions match and support each other, is one type.

Correspondence truth is basically what authoritative doctrine states and what most everyone believes, is another.

Pragmatic truth is the truth that works for the individual, group or me.

In the realm of the Venn diagram, a forth truth, what I have referred to in the past as leakage, called adherent truth is that section of overlap between the other three truths.

These leakages or adherent truth's, are in my opinion: the primary reason driving this work; a primary operating premise of my thinking process, and really all reasonable thinking processes, and the very basis for all other thinking process!

Unknown

I would venture to say that for all we have uncovered, discovered, invented, and/or imagined, the known and knowable factors of our universe are miniscule compared to the unknown and unknowable.

This fact alone has caused us as a specie to have become, for more than half the population, in search for something outside ourselves to sustain us.

Well; it's not working, the external force(s) that they depend on to make everything all right, each group, of course having their own spin on what's right, are not fulfilling their function.

For what ever reason, half or a small majority of the population have risen to the top of the food chain, so to speak.

As an aside, or maybe not, maybe the whole point of this work, discourse, diary or journal, by what ever name:

I am a Deist; by definition, the belief that the truth about the existence of God can be discovered by the individual through the evidence of reason and nature without resort to religion or revelation.

My personal spin on the above is that the creating force(s), God, set the initial conditions for the universe and initiated what our scientists call the 'big bang'.

I do not believe (I do not operate on the premise) that God is interactive with the creation, though I do advocate that the creator is the creation and the creation is the creator.

This has been touched on previously in this work and in my first one, and will be again and again, later!

The point I am trying to make is that the latest poll in the United States indicates that Deism or something liken to it is the operating principle of about half the population, and the other, lager half covers the range for God to do good things by answering prayers, to a God that is so interactive that instant retribution, to say nothing of eternal fire to go along with charity and grace.

The next reflects once again what I have said over and over again, probably too often, but it is a very deep part of how and why I think as I do.

I personally believe or disbelieve nothing.

I am finite, and the universe(s) is/are infinite.

I do not have available to me enough date to discern the 'absolute truth' or even any truth.

I know that I cannot operate in this mode, so I have developed operating premise's contrived of limited data, filtered through my hereditary subconscious and/or cultural subconscious, filtered through my parochial bias, that are often situation oriented, and that they may overlap or even contradict each other.

Once again I know that I have said this over and over, but I have also stated that each section of this work should be able to stand alone, so the reiteration should be acceptable to the patient reader, and I expect only the patient reader has gotten this far, thank you.

Because of the above, my reason and rationale are dependent on what I 'know', and the vast 'unknown and unknowable' that for me are behind an opaque veil that I do not and probably will not ever have access.

In a word I operate on what I know (or think that I know?).

I know that the hells on this earth are no part and parcel of some external forces.

Our troubles are our own and we will have to solve them, by realizing as a whole population, that the creative force(s) are not interactive, but that the initial conditions of the beginning have/ will allow us to evolve into a species that can live in harmony and live to get off this rock before it is consumed by the suns' nova.

I will try not to beat you with this theme in the future, but for what ever reason, I do not consciously control every thing that comes from the point of my pencil.

Victim

Victim is a word with unpleasant connotations that is used to describe persons or a person that has suffered a debilitating mishap at the hands of another, others, accidents, acts of God/or for God, and natural disasters.

Statistically everyone has a fair possibility of being a victim at least once in their lifetime, and more often when looked at from the/a universal prospective.

Barring unpreventable accidents (?), and acts of God (natural disasters), most people are victimized by others, either in or out of their community.

Are we prone to be victims, or is the very nature of our species to make victims of others for our own gain?

A broad based 'collateral damage' across activities, even other than war, seem to be the excepted (?) norm.

Though and old cliché, we still climb to our various successes over the back of others.

We are competitive, both by training and nature, both genetically (survival of the fittest), and culturally (we start training our children to be competitive as soon as they can walk).

Although we preach sharing and cooperation, it is overridden by the need to be first, have more, or at least keep up with the Joneses.

In what ever area of the social order (?) our own endeavor must cover the issues better than anyone else, and this is the phenomena that leads even religions that believe in the same God to go to war in the most barbaric and ungodly manner.

It seems to be the same with governments, business and most personal endeavors.

We are so consumed with me, mine, and my better idea, plan or point of view, that a majority of our personal and national resources are consumed in this drive for superiority.

Throughout history man has developed great tools to solve these conflicts in a logical and reasonable manner i.e., the dialectic and diplomacy.

For what ever reason these wonderful tools are not used often enough and conflict ensues and often ends in a situation where might equals right.

We don't call it this, we tell ourselves that each of us, on both sides of the conflict are right; and the losers are the victims of the winners, and the cycle goes on in a wave like manner, the waxing and waning of the same forces on both sides that cause these conflicts.

My ideas and methods of life are better than yours, so for your own good I will at least send missionaries to convert you or soldiers to force you to come around to the right way of thinking.

You are with me or against me, you may/must convert or die, it is your choice, and to join us is the only way to save your soul.

And, once again I am back to my primary scold: the unreasonable belief in an interactive creative force that is on my side and is directing me to bring you to salvation.

This phenomenon is not only limited to religion, but to the various isms' that have risen and fallen throughout our history.

In a word, the human species has a propensity to need external forces to cope, when in reality, the answers are all internal to themselves.

Don't be or cause others to be victims, be true to thy self and produce more than you consume.

Let 'to each his own', be your bywords – as long as they stay out of your space??!!

Winner

Another facet of the human condition that I have mentioned before: Competition.

In competition, the basic goal is to be the winner, although some say it's not weather you win of loose that counts, but how well you played the game.

Then, associated with winner, the subject of this section, we find a trident effect i.e., the winner, the loser, and how well the individual(s) involved played the game.

Let's start at the bottom, the game, the competition itself.

What is it all about? – I have come to the conclusion that it is at least a substitute for war; and at best, a training tool for warriors.

If this is truly the case, then a large portion of human nature tends toward conflicts with others.

I have touched the area before, while alluding to the 'survival of the fittest', or our putting our children in athletic programs at a very young age.

What this section will try to look closer at is the result of these ideas and activities.

We have looked at the game and found it to be a blue print of how life works, should or will work.

Now let's look at the loser or losers.

In a marathon, where dozens, hundreds or even thousands participate, the losers, in most cases, those that finished won by the fact that they participated.

There doesn't seem to be a down side here, where large numbers are involved with the outcome to be no losers but still only one winner?

This is not the case; however, in team activities or one on one competitions.

Looking at the team concept, we find that it come is two phases, the whole team in competition with another team of the same size and make-up, and the team's members participating in a one on one competition with the other team, striving for a win or lose score.

Once again, in the one on one team competition, the losers of the individual contests on the winning team are still winners by association.

Now; on to the group team that operates as a whole against another group team.

From amateur, grade school, high school, collage, to professional sports, this team winning/losing concept is mostly judged by the cumulative season performance of the participating teams.

The losing team in any activity has outstanding players, who mostly go on to other winning teams in the future.

I think my point here is that the losers sooner or later drop out of the game.

Now; to the meat of this section, the winner!

In our society and perhaps the world over, the winner is king for a day, or in some cases for life.

In professional sports, the winners and/or stars receive great celebrity and monetary rewards.

In business, the leaders in what ever enterprise are also rewarded with vast material gains, to say nothing of personal pride and prestige.

To be a winner is to have power.

It comes to mind that the hereditary evolutionary phenomena of the survival of the fittest has been honed to even a finer degree in the cultural evolution.

It is not enough to just survive; the ultimate individual and social goal is to be the winner.

Out of this attitude seems to come most of humanities problems.

This driving force that allows us to thrive and prosper may also be the force that drives us to extinction.

Perhaps we should embrace the third prong of the trident; 'it matters not who won or lost but how we played the game'.

Maybe we should all take a page out of the pre-school teacher's handbook and all play nice.

Wisdom

When I think of wisdom, it is the middle prong of the trident of self actualization e.g., maturity, wisdom and oneness with the universe.

I will start this section with a caveat about all that has come before and all that will follow.

I know that I wander all over the place, all the time, during the session of each section, but that is the way I think, and is the very foundation of what I think and what I think about.

Life is complex, to say the least, and this presentation is the result of self examination and analysis, and to be truthful, must have free reign.

This may never be seen by another, but if it is, that other should and must understand what this study, representation, or what ever is all about.

With that said, probably not for the first time, or the last time, now back to this section, wisdom.

This was the last section written, but due to the arbitrary alphabetic arrangement of this work, it may seem slightly out of context?

I hope that myself and anyone else exposed to this work are able to observe it in a holistic manner, as a totality, a multi cellular entity, if you will, rather than a hand full of random cells.

The above is directly related to the theme of this section.

To achieve wisdom, from my perspective, I must have or must reach or be mature, and from my point of view maturity entails the bringing together the maximization of my capabilities, while realizing and minimizing my limitations, but still maximizing the output of these parameters.

For me, maturity, or what ever maturity I have achieved, came when I realized that as a person I have a personal space that was mine and mine alone, and in order to function properly, that space had to be protected.

Lo and behold, I will be recognized and respected.

Do I think wisdom will come when I find out how to use the new concept of my personal space, my recognition and my respect?

Step one, others have a personal space!

Enter the Golden Rule: "Do unto others as you would have done to you".

Recognition is a two way street, in order to be recognized, you must recognize others and their personal space.

Enter the Enlightenment: "All men are created equal".

Learn to respect both of the above quoted concepts.

That is my version of maturity.

Wisdom is, "How the hell do I do that"?

An as an aside, Oneness with the universe is when you answer that question properly!

Xenophobia

Xenophobia: The fear, disgust, distrust, hate, adrenaline driven reaction to strangers?

Some dictionaries define it as: Zen o phobe, a person or society/culture unduly fearful or contemptuous of strangers or foreigners or foreign ideas or cultures, especially as reflected in their political, religious or cultural views.

I don't think either of the above descriptions/definitions of the phenomena is correct or complete?

We seem, as a species, to have some abhorrence toward all other subspecies that make up the whole of the human race, and beyond that, any extraterrestrials that might happen into/onto our world.

I will begin this section with an idea that we may be right, and why.

Throughout history, when ever one social group came upon another, one or the other was subdued or at least altered, and one or the other more or less had power over the other.

One of my most used or abused concepts, 'power'!

There seems to be in the nature of the Homo Sapiens the need to have a whipping boy; some one to look down on or lord over.

It didn't/doesn't seem to help matter that the species as a whole has a color range from pink/white of the Caucasian to the near jet black of the Negro, and every shade in between.

Along side this, until very recently each culture was attached to each skin color, so that when two cultures crossed paths there would have been a good change that they looked different from each other.

In most cases the male of the species will/would mate with any female whatever and the females often found to different species male to be attractive, and this could have caused some unrest from both sides of the isle.

Overriding this, something that just recently been recognized in human nature, we exude pheromones, just like the other animal species.

In the human cases, at least, these pheromones sent a message between individuals that they could mate without worrying about any incestuous problem with their offspring.

I a word, the pheromones communicated the message; 'Let's make beautiful babies'!

As you can see, the above issues could have caused a jealousy problem in that first contact.

As an aside, in later, past and present times this exchanging of females from one group to another was used to bring the groups together in friendship, or at least some form of cooperation and lessening of cross group tensions.

I would assume that early on, when groups traveled little, the shading problem didn't arise?

There seems to have been a period in the Mediterranean Sea area, where all the societies seemed to have equally sophisticated and the color barrier was overlooked equal status of all involved.

This didn't seem to cause a lessening in conflict and war, but the reasons don't seem to me to have been associated with xenophobia, but more a struggle for resources, with a sometimes religious conversion overtone.

Not until later, when world travel and travel into the interior of the continents did these sophisticated cultures come in contact with savages, cultures that had not reached their level of sophistication, or that had degenerated, for what ever reason to the savage state.

Even in the relatively overall sameness of cultures, there have been conflicts, wars of great magnitude, and merging of cultures, through empire building.

Civilization (city dwelling, by definition), so to speak, has evolved in the cultural sphere.

But still, in each city there were neighborhoods of different ethnic, social and religious groups that lived in relative harmony.

There was some strife, certainly, but it was strife more or less among equals.

It wasn't until contact with the savages that the cultural quality came to the fore.

These savages were surly subhuman and could not have the same status of real people, and the cultural balance became skewed to such and extent that xenophobia once again became a prime factor in cultural relationships, if it had ever really been subdued by the civilization process.

For what ever reason, the phenomena has waxed and waned over the centuries until now it is part and parcel of our collective parochial bias.

The global economic system that has a life of its own, on the one hand, and being driven from some societies and/or governments will never bear sweet fruit until our collective cultures have evolved to such an extent that xenophobia among our races and cultures and/or societies is eliminated.

How we, as a race/species will resolve this issue is the balance point of whether we will ever get off this rock and spread the species throughout the galaxy and universe.

To paraphrase Ben Franklin, 'gentlemen if we don't hang together, we will die together'.

Yoda

The idea of the 'Force' is strong in my nature.

There have been untold numbers of books written about magic powers of every sort, and the very science that has allowed the technical revolution that we live in has at it basis in alchemy, a magic process to turn lead into gold; a weak coverage of alchemy, but I am sure you, the reader, get the picture.

The supernatural has been a part of the human condition from the very beginning of our cultures; artifacts from small images to wall paintings, to large images, buildings and all other icons dedicated to some external force(s).

My question; to myself, is this phenomena a drive to have external forces aid and abet our survival or is it a search from within ourselves to understand and overcome nature?

To keep it simple, I will compare theism and deism, two of the belief systems about the creating force(s) – God.

For the most part, the theists advocates that God, in one or more forms, can be, and is involved interactively in the lives of the believers, and is the cause of all creation, and the controlling factor in the overall lives of all creatures in the universe.

This God is capable of, and does bypass the otherwise fixed natural laws to make miracles to benefit those in this particular belief system, even to the point of communications with prophets to pass his word to the rest of the people.

And most of all, at some point, at the end of days, all the good believers will go to heaven and live with God, and all the rest will languish in some limbo or eternal Hell Fire.

The Deist, on the other hand, in simple context, advocates that the creating force(s) is/are a Grand Cosmic Phenomena that created the universe(s) by setting the initial conditions that allowed the forming of the universe(s) and the set of natural laws that it entails, that allowed for the evolution the stars, galaxies, and in a later time our Solar System and earth.

On Earth, life began, evolved and has come to this point in our existence.

But the outcome is/was not pre-destined!

The various operations of the converting of energy to matter and back again, over and over, seemingly to a more complex state are deterministic, in that there are certain parameters in these activities that allow some variation in the result, within that fixed parameter.

I (we?) call these parameters the natural laws.

A sample of these parameters in action is our free will, also operational within certain parameters, within the boundaries of the natural laws themselves.

In our lifetime we make untold numbers of decisions, hopefully based on reasonable evaluation of the capabilities and limitations of the resources and the situation at hand.

Our lives are deterministic, in that we will be born and we will die, but the duration and activities of our lifetime is not pre-destined, but driven by the free will decisions we make personally, combined with the decisions of others, that are not in our control.

Given all the above, I may not have made it clear what the difference between the Theist and Deist is from the point of view of my operating premise.

My premise is simple, the Theists God interacts and tweaks the system, while the Deist God set it in motion, and does not interact.

Now, at last, back to Yoda, and the 'Force'.

There is something, seemingly, in our nature that more or less drives us to control our own destiny.

Although I can't and don't find that I have any control of the 'Force', I have no doubt what so ever that the 'Force' is with me.

I have touched on the next, before and will do so again, I am sure.

The Creator is the Creation and the Creation is the Creator.

This seemingly circular statement is very clear and understandable within my personal representation, but I have yet been able to find the word to express it better.

Maybe that is what all my writing is about, to find a way to express it.

Zen

I have wrestled with the very meaning of the word and the concept of Zen.

One dictionary definition alludes to finding Enlightment through introspection, which I interpret to mean an internal search for the answer to your questions. I question the ability for one to do this with out external input, so that definition didn't help me to grasp the Zen concept?

The first contact, on my part, was to Zen Buddhism, and as time goes on I see books about the Zen of everything from applesauce to the Zen of Zen.

I have come to the conclusion that it has something to do with achieving oneness with the subject at hand, and to fine the zone of the particular activity involved.

This section will try to develop the paths that I have taken to grasp the Zen concept.

My first pass; it came to me while trying to go to sleep one night, to analyze, atomize, digitize the subject at hand.

To digitize, I feel is to discover the smallest unit available and observe it as a discrete and static entity.

But when I get there, I remember the story about pictures in the newspaper. If you magnify them highly there is nothing there but a lot of black, white, and grey dots liken to the pixels on the television or computer screen.

Then I think of an old cliché, don't look too close!

So digitize, using my definition, does not seem to work here.

Next: to atomize, or break down to the smallest element, the subject at hand.

When one has the elements isolated, what does one analyze them against, each other for internal comparison or external, for a world view?

If I use external elements, can I be sure they are relevant to the internal ones?

I am going nowhere and finding myself thinking of a Zen Kong-an statement, 'If you open your mouth you die, if you keep your mouth shut, you are already dead', what does that mean?

I have discovered, for my self at least, that the above means that in some situations, shut up and in other instances you must speak up, remembering; however, that you can talk yourself into more trouble than you can talk yourself out of.

Therefore; if this is true, the secret to the Zen of a given subject is that different responses are necessary for different situations, and that when I figure those out, I will have matured, gained wisdom, become enlightened and/or have become one with the universe.

Basically, this means to me, that my internal system, unconscious, sub conscious, and conscious activities filtered through my parochial bias and real time external events present me with a situation solution that I can or cannot react too in the manner presented, by the exercise of my free will.

I will go, or have gone into free will in greater detail elsewhere in this presentation, but in a word, a thought or action comes to mind and through the exercise of free will I veto the action or go through with it.

Therefore, I conclude that the Zen of a subject (life or whatever?), is the exercise of my free will on whatever aspect is presented.

What is the sound of one hand clapping?, slap the table!

Synoposis And Conclusion

I am, with mixed emotion, at the end of the analysis and data gathering phase of the operation.

My problem now, is when I finish this section, should it remain at the end as it was written, or should it be presented first, with all the rest in footnote notation?

At this point I don't have the answer to this question.

To do a proper synopsis and conclusion I must reiterate much of the preamble of my previous work, 'How and Why Do I Think as I Do?', and then to on from there.

It has already been touched on in the various sections presented in this work, but I think now that I may have better understanding of what I was trying to at the onset of these works over two years ago?

I am finite, and the universe, for all practical purposes, infinite.

The only way to have absolute truth or to embrace core reality is to have all the data that goes into those concepts.

Being finite in an infinite universe, I will never have this complete data set.

Therefore, I cannot believe or disbelieve anything!

Also, I cannot function in that situation!

I must gather and categorize my available data, filter it through my evolved unconscious and subconscious systems, and again through my parochial bias, that data base laid down in my formative years, usually stated as before one is five years old, that was input with no buffers of previous input, and bring all this to my pre-frontal cortex and merge it with real time, on line inputs and cognize it with the mental representations that take the form of operating premise.

To use the vernacular, what I think and what I believe or disbelieve are just operating premises, and not representations of the truth or core reality.

They are my unique point of view, compiled of all the data that I have gathered and stored, real time input, and filtered through my parochial bias.

With this in mind, I will now get to the synopsis, the gathering and categorizing the data presented in this work, and the conclusion I have or will have drawn from it.

Synopsis; by definition, is a brief summary or abstract.

I have tried to write this work, mostly in the first person, find my self writing, 'you, we, they, etc', and also a lot of 'I, me, my and myself', I hope you can grasp the each of those pronouns are addressed to some facet of myself, because, at the bottom, this work is about me.

Also, this work is about demes and different points of view and modus operandi.

It is I, as a deme of one; I, as one among many (or few) in a deme, and all the other demes in the world.

In summary, all the individuals or groups in a deme don't necessarily act or think the same way about the same or all issues.

This is the bedrock and/or foundation of most or all of the worlds' conflicts.

In abstract, this work is a critique of all the other demes that don't agree with what I think, and this is what I think about most.

Is it a summation by a hubristic and perhaps also an ego/ megalomaniac personality, pointing the finger at all the wrongs of those other guys?

After Thoughts

What do I think about what I think?

First, I am totally convinced that that what I think and what I say here will have no effect on the outcome of this universal saga that I have called the creator and creation as one.

Second, it doesn't even bother me, because just having the ability and opportunity to say it is enough.

In the section on Soul, I described my interpretation of what the Soul was and how it worked. If there is any truth in my interpretation, then at the end of days, or this creation, if there is a judgment, my Soul, as a data base, will be read and judged, and the creating force(s) will (if not already), then be aware of my attempt to add another (my) point of view to the process and to produce more than I consumed.

Well, I guess that's it, except for a few basic thoughts, that are liken to seeds in the garden of my mind:

On free will; free will is the ability of the pre-frontal cortex to veto, in real time, the/a potential action or thought that has been run through the various unconscious and subconscious systems by having, through parallel processing, a 500 ms preview of the data. Enough time for the latest external data to be analyzed and operated on.

Neural synapses are not just transfer points in the data stream, but are also storage points for data bits, activated by the buildup of concurrent like labeled potentials that collectively bring for synaptic activity.

Human pheromones and their power to change the inner attitude and direct it toward procreation is through a connection to DNA/RNA non kin relationships

Stay in the philosophic mode – per ZEN – let it go, put it all down – Translation? : The senses absorb the external input, but the mind builds the representation. Use the representation while meditating and/or philosophizing and shut off the externals. It's all in your mind?

When dealing with the truth and beliefs there have been many routes taken to describe and/or capture the essence of these phenomena. I have taken the two I found most enlightening and merged them into a personal representation of how to ascertain the available truths. Visualize the graphic symboligy of an equilateral triangle with each of the points representing one of the three types of truth systems available to us:

Cohesive, correspondent and pragmatic, defined, in order, cohesive; those truths that align themselves with other known and experimentally proven truths, correspondent; the truths espoused by authority figures or organizations and what most people believe, and pragmatic; those truths that work for me in a given situation that work to my advantage e.g., business is business. With the above in mind, now picture a Venn diagram, the universal set is absolute truth/core reality and the three subsets, A, B, and C, represent the three types of truth. With the over lap of the three subsets, you will notice a small section in the center of the overlap that contains part of each of the other three. This is the universal set leaking through, the subset that is called adherent truth. This may be the nearest finite man can get to infinite truth! [Source: Annals of the New York Academy of Sciences Volume 901, "Complexity IX. Closure over the Organization of a Scientific Truth" by Jerry L.R. Chandler]

As is the Force, the dichotomy is strong in me; digital vs analog, right brain vs left brain, discrete vs continuous and free will vs predestination, a forever and always operation that has been defined as the dialectic, from thesis vs antithesis to synthesis, with the synthesis as the new thesis, ad infinitum.

To me Post Modernism is very Zen. There is no reality except in the mental construct, as science is just a point of view, as are the various religions. Each facet of each culture is as valid as any other. Don't judge a man until you have walked a mile in his moccasins, and then don't judge him at all. Perhaps a little simplistic and vague description, but that's all I can get from it.

Has the 'Bambi' syndrome, and other anthro-animalistic movies and TV caused more vegan/vegetarians, and with the lack of complex animal carbohydrates causing an epigenic decline in the species?

Political forces and directions are the result of what I call the Political Trident: three different primary demes in any elected body of representatives; Manifest Destiny or global nationalism, Pragmatic Economics or what best works for me/us (usually in the short term), and the religious right or left. In the case that two or all of these demes come together that is the political direction of the entity. When one or the other falters, the direction changes and/or the entity temporarily becomes stagnate or vacillates, and in many case looses effectiveness.

Diminishing scale implies that things happen in cycles, thus classical physics, to quantum physics, to sub-particle (meta-quantum physics) or non-quantum physics (meta/sub). Perhaps this phenomena will pass from determinate (classical) to uncertainty (quantum), back to determinate (meta/sub quantum), to mini-micro (determinate) to micro/chaotic/complex, uncertainty to macro (non-determinate)?

Is there a correlation between Ant caste changes (delta) and the global economy? As the changes (delta) in job placement i.e., out sourcing and manufacturing plant movement.

Another view of the 80/20 heuristic, as operating in the body politic of America: 40% in the theist spiritual bent, 40% in the deist secular bent, and 20%, the independents, vacillating, some where between, and often their vote makes policy. Is this another aspect of a political trident?

A solution to some or most of the world's problems could be an international treaty to have international treaties to cover each individual States particular problem(s), from the point of view of what the rest of the world could/can/will do to help alleviate this/ those problems and what the particular State can do to help itself. If this sounds like the U.N., it's not, the U.N seems to be a catch up operation and not a preventative one!

The configuration of the time tube sets the parameters the deterministic, but not pre-destined path of life through time. As the individual number of entities increases, within a given section of the tube, chaos ensues. Multicellular entities should/will be encased with single representation membranes to alleviate this chaos.

Given the Brahman Bucket of blood, the caldron that hold all souls as drops of blood and the spider web like entities that connect them: a soul that holds all of the data received through life has the potential to read any soul who spiders webs cross and/or his own soul?

A simple scenario of the beginning of life could be: a hydro carbon bubble formed around a crystal formation and carbon nanotubes formed and permeated the hydrocarbon bubble between the interior of the package and the exterior allowing toxins to be secreted to the exterior and new resources brought back into the package, through the polar ends of the nanotubes being reversed?

First the crystalline formation becomes encased in a hydrocarbon bubble, importing resources and exporting toxins (oxygen, etc), through several level of non-life until emerging processes (?) from each level reach the critical mass that is life. The DNA is a remnant of these first crystals.

An autocatalytic system, natural bubbles, autocatalytic nanotubes build geodesticdome type lattice with nanotube input/output perpendicular to inner surfaces, oxidation, autopoiesis, and think extraterrestrial amino acids in nature.

A neodeist perspective: The creative force(s), in the vernacular; God, in not interactive, the creator is the creation, and due to perfection of the creation, has no need to tweak the system.

Each and every discrete and static point consists of the history of all other discrete/static points previous to its self and/but represents only one of the many possible discrete/static points that the collective history could have produced. Think of dialectic tree from the past to the present, where each synthesis became a new thesis.

Is instinct hereditary memory e.g., how and when a bird builds its nest, and if so how much hereditary memory is available for other things i.e., intuition, cognation, creativity, extrapolation and/or innovation, and if not, what signals from nature initiate genetic action (turns on genes) to allow these phenomena, if that is what happens?

Special Last Note:

If any of the subjects in this section, or any other, for that matter, don't seem complete or even relevant or redundant, it's because this section, any maybe all the other sections, are works in progress, again, seeds, if you will.

About the Author

Born in the middle of the Depression, a jack of all trades before dropping out of high school in 1950 to join the Navy for 4 years. Graduated from high school and had the opportunity to accept a scholarhip to MIT or the US Coast Guard Academy, but did not accept. Did 5 years in civilian life picking up more trades before going into the Air Force for 7 years. Went to college in the 70's, and joined the Mensa Society in the 80's. A 15-year career with Computer Language Research in Carrollton, TX, retiring in 1992. Now living in a primitive camp in North Texas High Country.